Generation Of Opportunity

Published by Pastoral Educational Services
(National Educational Programs for Vocations)

Executive Director: Rev. Thomas E. Comber, C.S.P.
Coordinating Director of Pastoral Services: Joseph W. Nash
21 Harristown Road, Glen Rock, New Jersey 07452

Consultants:
Rev. James A. Viall
*President of the National Conference of
Diocesan Vocation Directors
Vocation Director for
the Diocese of Cleveland*

Rev. William C. Clark
*Assistant Vocation Director,
Archdiocese of Newark*

Design: Edward R. Wade
Photographic Consultant: Ken Wittenberg

Nihil Obstat:
V. Rev. Msgr. John H. Koenig, S.T.L.
Censor Librorum

Imprimatur:
+ Thomas A. Boland, S.T.D.
Archbishop of Newark, N.J.

February 5, 1968

The Nihil Obstat and Imprimatur are official declarations
that a book or pamphlet is free of doctrinal or moral error.
No implication is contained therein that those who have
granted the Nihil Obstat and Imprimatur agree with the
contents, opinions or statements expressed.

Generation of Opportunity

BY GEORGE FISCHER

CONTENTS

	PAGE	CHAPTER
WE ASKED WHY	4	1
NINE ANSWERS	7	2
GREATEST REWARDS	9	3
ADVICE TO YOUNG MEN	15	
CHALLENGES TODAY AND TOMORROW	22	
CELIBACY AND LOVE	31	
BETWEEN SUNDAYS	35	
RELEVANCE OF ACTION	43	
BROTHERS' REPORT	49	
WHY SHE BECAME A SISTER	57	1
CONVENT OBSTACLES	61	1
ON THE JOB AND OFF	65	1
ADVICE TO YOUNG WOMEN	68	1
ADVICE TO PARENTS	73	1
A PRACTICAL APPROACH	77	1
INVITATION TO ACTION	81	

We Asked Why

"Honestly I do not know."

"I had a strong desire to say Mass."

"I was about to get married, but decided to give God a chance. That was 47 years ago."

"I was an insurance agent. But I came to realize there was a greater insurance needed."

"I just had to try it."

These are some of the answers from all kinds of priests, brothers and sisters across the country and some Americans serving in Africa and Asia, including Vietnam who generously answered the question "why?" Why become a priest? Why a brother? Why a sister?

That is what this book is all about. Instead of putting the question to one or two and getting one or two individual responses, this question is answered by hundreds to get a *composite* picture of religious life today. The composite results of this query to 2,000 priests, 1,000 brothers and 5,000 sisters offer a broad view of what religious life is, why people enter it and what they do in it. The "why" of the priesthood is answered by 200 priests in this first section of the book. The "why" of the brotherhood is covered by 100 brothers in chapter 9. And answers to the same questions about the sisterhood are given by 500 sisters in the second section. Then all answers are brought together for parents in the third section with advice of interest to all.

A clearer general understanding of the "why" of a religious career is *the* reason for this book. The collecting and grouping of hundreds of opinions from those already in a religious career help us to understand what is important about this life. Some respondents in the survey make comments about their lives that could be considered discouraging. These honest expressions of priests, brothers and sisters may encourage some readers and discourage others.

What is its importance? If that question could be answered in a satisfying sentence which would apply to every priest, brother or sister, there would have been no need for a survey. Instead, the answer lies in a mix of many factors and this book attempts to summarize the important ones. Generally, one common characteristic of those who participated in the survey is a deeply felt, unselfish love. Their responses show this. They also indicate, in many cases, a virtue and dedication to a way of life that few understand.

A word of caution is in order concerning the graphs and percentages reported in this book. The grouping of opinions and other answers from priests, brothers and sisters does not imply airtight compartments. The percentages given are merely broadbrush indications and not scientifically precise; they do not need to be.

To understand the life of a priest a little better, let us first take a look at why 200 priests undertook this career and what they report they are getting out of it.

PRIEST VOCATION
INFLUENCE

EXAMPLE OF A PRIEST	**44%**	
DESIRE TO HELP	**27%**	
EXAMPLE OF FAMILY	**18%**	
SPIRITUAL REASONS	**15%**	
ALWAYS WANTED TO BE	**10%**	
EXAMPLE OF NUNS	**8%**	
SELF IMPROVEMENT	**8%**	
MISSIONARY ZEAL	**1.5%**	
VOCATION APPEAL	**1.5%**	

Of all the above influences a third of the priests give more than one answer,
bringing the total to 133 percent. The responses are ranked by frequency of mention.

Nine
Answers

Bishops and priests are much like most career men trying to answer the question why they are where they are today. Ask a mathematician, physicist, engineer, doctor or any professional man why he undertook that particular career and he will probably give you statements similar in many ways to those in the chart.

The answers from priests across the country fall into nine categories.

1. *Example.* This influences more young men than any other factor — the example of another priest, his friendliness and enthusiasm. At least 44 percent of the priests remember this as their most important influence when they decided to enter a seminary. A priest from Massachusetts recalls that he spent two years getting to know priests before he decided to try the priesthood himself. A pastor in Fort Lauderdale, Florida, writes, "An

older priest talked to me about the good I could do." A priest in St. Paul, Minnesota, got to know priests through his job as sacristan at a college chapel "which kept me there two hours a day."

Having some social contact with priests, then, represents one of the most important reasons why young men become interested in the priesthood — interested enough, that is, to try it themselves. Yet, according to the survey, about 38 percent of the priests today do not have any contact with young people or for some reason —the nature of their work and the lack of time — do not have the social opportunities to spend time with young Catholic men.

2. *Service.* Second in the minds of most priests as they recall what influenced them to enter the seminary is a strong personal desire to serve and help others. In the words of one priest, 27 percent indicate they had "a desire to do something more

worthwhile" than what they were actually doing or thought they would do with their careers.

A Jesuit from Philadelphia remembers, "The thought of a vocation really got strong during naval service in World War II. Basically, I thought I would like to help kids through the rough years of adolescence and young adulthood." This priest now is a student counselor and popular retreat master.

Another Pennsylvanian, a 34-year-old diocesan priest, says he too was looking for something worth doing . . . "a real dreadful feeling of waste if I considered just making money." He worked at other professions for a while, was ordained at the age of thirty and says he is happy teaching high school.

3. *Family.* Third in the list of reasons why priests today say they entered the seminary is their own family background and training. About 18 percent attribute their vocations to the fact that they came from homes where the priesthood was held in high regard.

A Franciscan from Kansas City remembers with enthusiasm that he came from "a wonderful religious home." A pastor in Louisville, Kentucky, writes that it was the "encouragement of a good mother and father, the prayers of both and the interest of a good pastor."

4. *Spiritual.* Fourth among the why's is a spiritual reason and one out of six priests, about 16 percent, mentions this. Writes one priest from Miami, Florida, "It is the only way I thought I could save my own soul while praying to save others."

Spiritual reasons are not the same for everyone. A Redemptorist in Brooklyn, New York, plainly admits he had a strong desire to offer Mass. He cannot understand why people look for answers to vocations "with six syllable words. Our Lord didn't give long-winded answers." Thomas Merton's book, "Seven Storey Mountain," provided the spiritual inspiration to a young priest in Nashville, Tennessee. "It led me to the conviction that happiness is proportional to sanctity," he writes.

There are five other, less frequently mentioned answers to the question, "Why did I become a priest?" 5. Some ten percent state they "always wanted to be a priest since early grade school." 6. The influence and example of the teaching sisters in grade school account for eight percent of the answers. That means that sisters could claim credit for inspiring about one out of twelve or approximately 4,500 priests. 7. By projecting the results of the survey, the same number could attribute their decision on the priesthood to self-improvement reasons. The priesthood, according to these kinds of responses, offered these men an opportunity to become better persons socially, intellectually, materially and spiritually.

The last two answers for becoming a priest, according to the priests of today, represent only 1.5 percent of all the factors mentioned. 8. A desire to do missionary work, specifically, is one major influence on the vocations of 15 out of every thousand priests. 9. The response to "clergy vocational talks" directed at selected candidates was a similar number of vocations.

About ten percent of the priests who participated in the survey are over 60 years of age and about ten percent are under thirty. The remaining 80 percent are evenly divided in their thirties, forties and fifties. They have an average of 16 years in the priesthood and total over 2,900 years, almost enough to reach clear back in time to Melchisedech — the Old Testament priest who first offered bloodless sacrifices and who is recalled in the prayers of every Mass celebrated.

Celebrating Mass, incidentally, is only one of the rewards priests today say they enjoy as a result of their vocation decision. Let us examine what they consider to be the rewards of the priesthood in the next chapter.

Greatest Rewards

"Knowing you have helped persons, not just glossing over problems but helping people understand themselves is the greatest reward," writes a 30-year-old priest from Milwaukee.

"I honestly don't think in terms of rewards," reflects a 39-year-old priest from Philadelphia, "but certainly the offering of the Sacrifice of the Mass is the highest point of my day."

"The greatest reward of the priesthood is hopefully eternal *life*," figures a priest from Fargo, North Dakota, who underscores the word, "life."

The greatest rewards, according to the priest responses, seem to offset the challenges and problems brought up in the survey. The priests were not asked what they considered to be their greatest privilege or honor. The statement to be completed was: "The greatest reward of the priesthood is:" They could answer it in their own words and with as many words as they wished. The responses, then, reflect what priests themselves feel they are getting out of the priesthood, not a recital of status or honors.

The greatest rewards fall into four categories. In the order of those most frequently mentioned, the opportunity to help others is first, finding self-fulfillment is next, celebrating Mass and administering the sacraments is third, and the spiritual reward or promise of eternal life is fourth.

Half the priests surveyed regard the opportunity to help others in any way they can as their greatest reward. Most see that their function of serving others is best performed through some kind of organized effort. They know they can help others as individuals because within themselves they have a feeling for other people. But, say the priests, the organization of "parish," instruction programs of many kinds, "people-oriented programs such as the Christian Family Movement," and the general backing of the Catholic Church all add authority and effectiveness to what they are trying to do.

One priest from Wilmington, Delaware, feels that his function in the parish makes him "able to give people some peace of mind and heart in this confusing world in the face of suffering and hardship."

Many of the comments are similar across the country. Another priest in Davenport, Iowa, feels that priests are "in a position to help people help themselves both in relation to God and to their fellowmen." *As a layman he does not think he would be in a position to help people as effectively as he can now.*

While most priests talk about helping people in life, some, like the one from San Diego, mention the good priests can do in death. "The greatest reward as I see it," this priest writes, "is the knowledge that periodically we can add something to some lives — and deaths."

The second greatest reward, mentioned by 35 percent of the priests, is similar to the first category. It is more personal and has to do with fulfillment. It is evident that priests who consider their greatest reward in helping people find fulfillment in this help to humanity.

The fulfillment reasons are grouped from all the responses that mention the words, "satisfaction," "appreciation," "fulfillment," and other expressions close to those ideas. The satisfaction they talk about can be for almost any worthwhile reason — helping others, and spiritual functions such as Mass and the sacraments.

An older priest from Louisville, Kentucky, puts it this way, "My greatest reward is the satisfaction that comes from the privileges that the priest enjoys in bringing the gifts of God (Mass, sacraments) to man."

A younger Father of St. Joseph from Albuquerque, New Mexico, says his greatest reward is "happiness — and to keep our spirit very young." A Redemptorist writes about his "joy and happiness through a very unique way of loving." Others mention the beauty they see in life through the priesthood they are in.

Many young priests, in stating what they think

their greatest reward is, use highly contemporary terms in expressing their fulfillment. They say they are happy because they are "tuned in" or "turned on" to the "all around good" they can do as priests.

The third greatest reward according to the frequency of mentions in the survey can be categorized as spiritual. Only one out of eight priests specifically mentions a spiritual reward.

Some of the spiritual rewards, such as the one mentioned by a 34-year-old parish assistant in a small Pennsylvania town, reflect a "servant" outlook. He talks about being a "priestly witness" and adds, "Sounds corny and pious but that's it in a nutshell." Another assistant in Evansdale, Iowa, says it is "doing God's work in so many, many ways."

A Paulist Father, ordained just one year, says his greatest reward in the priesthood is "the wide-ranging opportunity to experience God in other people." A college professor says simply, "Saying Mass." He adds other rewards — "absolving sinners and teaching the way to salvation."

A young priest, from Macomb, Illinois, still in his twenties, perhaps summarizes the spiritual rewards mentioned by 12 percent of the priests. He writes, "The greatest reward of my priesthood is the celebration of the eucharist in the midst of a genuine Christian community which I believe we have in our town and to be able to do anything that contributes to a continuous building of that community."

A young Jesuit who is studying for a doctorate in economics at Vanderbilt University cites a more personal spiritual reward, "To me the priesthood is the most significant work in the world. Its reward is the aid which it offers to a deep personal experience of God."

The fourth greatest reward, according to another 12 percent of the priests, is the promise of eternal life. A priest from Chicago calls it walking in the footsteps of Our Lord. Another from Baltimore writes that eternal life is the biggest reward he is looking for while he helps others toward the same goal.

A Pennsylvania pastor summarizes this point of view with the statement, "The greatest reward of the priesthood is the peace of mind that comes

THE GREATEST
REWARD OF THE
PRIESTHOOD

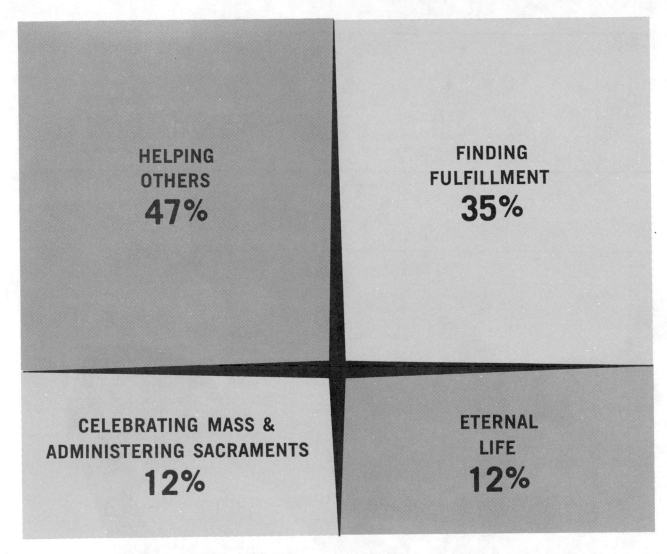

HELPING
OTHERS
47%

FINDING
FULFILLMENT
35%

CELEBRATING MASS &
ADMINISTERING SACRAMENTS
12%

ETERNAL
LIFE
12%

Percentage based on the opinion of 200 priests. Some
offered more than one reward, bringing the total to 106 percent.

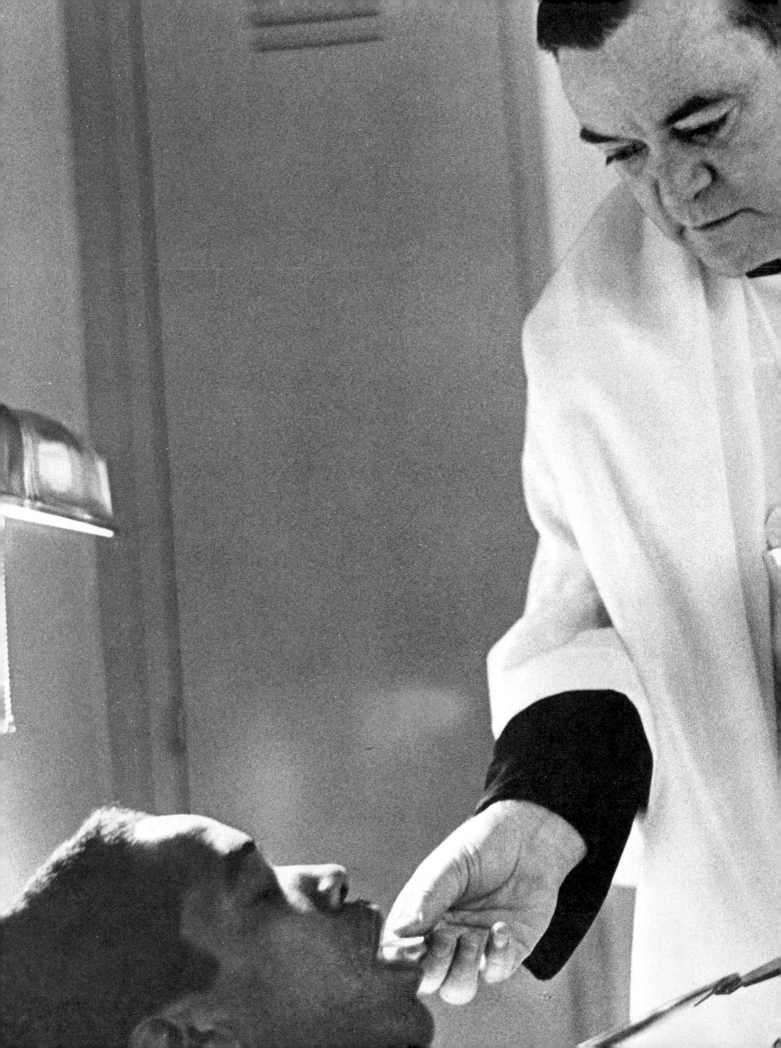

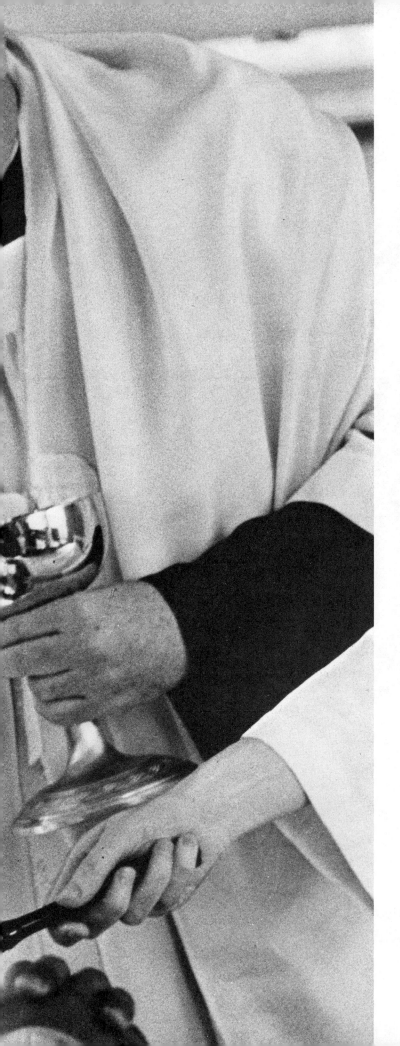

from the hope of eternal reward and from not having to care for the worldly needs of one's own self."

There are benefits here on earth, too. The priests are asked to judge the happiness and effectiveness of "most of the priests they know." The response is over 80 percent on the positive side. Over 62 percent feel that most priests are "effective and happy." Almost 20 percent are even more positive, rating most priests they know as "very effective and happy" or "effective and very happy." Only one out of eight priests tends toward the negative, ranking the priests they know as somewhat ineffective or unhappy. Six percent had no answer.

Another benefit is the opportunity for continued education after ordination. This is usually for obtaining some other professional goal. A priest from Philadelphia reports that any of the clergy who wish to continue their education have their tuition and expenses paid. A fourth of the priests state they have unlimited opportunities of all types, including summer school and clergy workshops. Another fourth indicate nearby colleges and universities are always available to priests for additional courses. About half of the priests indicate little or no opportunity for additional formal education. But with increasing demands on the priest as a professional man, they expect that the chances for additional education after the seminary will be better than 50-50 in the near future.

For some priests, rewards and benefits are not important. A Franciscan who works at the Cursillo training center in Kansas City, Missouri, says he is "not worried about that — the Lord will take care of that in due time."

Summary: Many reactions. How would priests advise young men considering the priesthood as a way of life? Their suggestions in the next chapter are interesting.

Advice To Young Men

Imagine yourself sitting in the center of a stage in an amphitheater surrounded by 200 priests. Each priest is there to tell you why (or why not) you should become a priest, and one by one, row by row, each priest will give you the best piece of advice he can.

After you listen to 200 comments, you would probably be confused. To avoid that problem, the advice to young men has already been jotted down on paper, grouped together and listed in nine different categories. These are the positive comments that priests give to young men. There are also negative comments — reasons why priests would discourage you from considering the priesthood as your career. These are grouped in six different categories.

First, let's take the positive advice.

Give yourself. Almost three out of ten priests say "Give yourself."

A priest from Greenville, South Carolina, writes, "1. — have a desire to give yourself completely.

2. — do not make any decisions until after two years. 3. — you do not need to decide before you enter the seminary. 4. — prayer and the Mass will give you courage, stamina, and the right intention."

Another priest from a suburban Milwaukee parish writes, "Be ready to dedicate your life wholeheartedly to something very special and extraordinary. Be prepared to love God and your fellowman intensely and be ready to pay any price to achieve this."

Try it. The comments of one out of six priests might be boiled down to two words — try it.

A priest in a small parish in Maplewood, Wisconsin, writes, "Give it a try. You will soon discover whether you can find yourself in this work. If you constantly feel like a stranger or that the ideals are out of your reach, then leave."

Another priest in Oakley, Kansas, puts it in a different way. He writes, "Give it a try and leave final decisions until later."

A Divine Word missionary from Duxbury, Massachusetts, says, "If you think you want to be

ENCOURAGEMENT
TO ENTER
THE SEMINARY

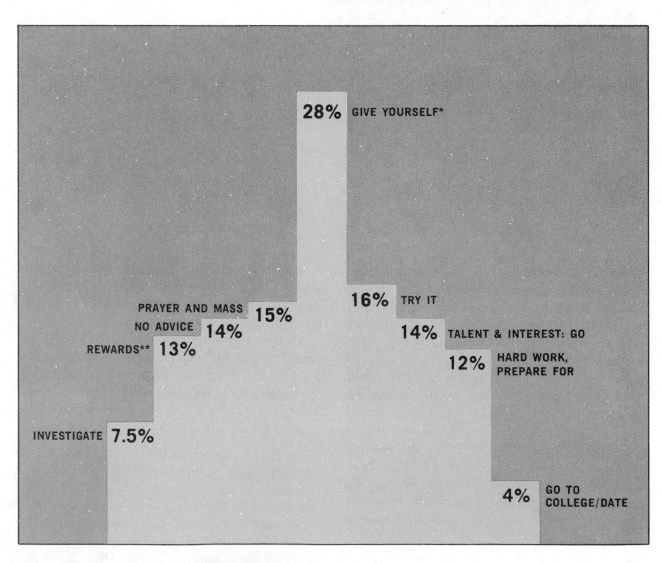

28% GIVE YOURSELF*

16% TRY IT

PRAYER AND MASS **15%**

NO ADVICE **14%**

REWARDS** **13%**

14% TALENT & INTEREST: GO

12% HARD WORK, PREPARE FOR

INVESTIGATE **7.5%**

4% GO TO COLLEGE/DATE

Basically this is the advice priest respondents give to young
men they encourage to enter the seminary. About a fourth give
more than one piece of advice, bringing the total to 123.5 percent.

* A third of these mention "sacrifice."

** Half of these mentioned
"personal sanctity."

a priest, go to the seminary to find out if you can make it."

Prayer and Mass. Another one out of six priests urges a program of prayer and regular attendance at Mass. A young priest who works in the diocese and chancery at Albany, New York, writes, "Learn theology well, especially scripture and learn to think for yourself while being obedient. Don't lose touch with the real world — and pray like crazy."

No Advice. About 14 percent of the priests say they don't have any advice for you because they don't feel qualified to counsel on what is a highly individual and personal matter. Many of these priests feel it is such a personal thing that you have to figure it out for yourself.

Seminary. Another 14 percent of the priests advise you to go to the seminary. They say not to worry about it so much — things will work out.

Rewards. Some 13 percent say the rewards are great in spite of all the problems you will encounter. A preaching priest from the Green Bay diocese says that "it's a great way of life and you can continue the fine Christian work and enjoy it at the same time."

Many priests cited the hundred fold reward mentioned in the famous text of Mark 10:29: "Truly, I say to you, there is no one who has left house or brothers or sisters or mother or father or children or lands, for my sake and for the gospel who will not receive a hundredfold now in this time, houses and brothers and sisters and mothers and children and lands, with persecutions, and in the age to come eternal life." That promise carries the authority of Christ himself.

Hard Work. One out of eight priests would remind you that the preparation for the life of a priest is very hard work.

Look Around. About seven percent of the priests encourage you to investigate. Look around for the diocese or the religious order that you feel would suit you best. This means examining your interests concerning the type of work you would like to do. If you like to be with people, generally help others, inquire about the new pastoral programs in your diocese: parishes are changing fast with up-to-date social action programs. If you are inclined toward the medical profession, there are religious orders which specialize in the medical field. If you are inclined toward teaching, find a good teaching organization whose program matches your ideas and ideals.

College First. And finally, four percent of the priests say go to college first, have fun in a normal social and athletic life. A Trappist in California feels that you "should have at least two years of college which normally means a broad acquaintance with life. Once you decide to go into the seminary, stay for at least one year even if it seems likely to kill you. But come home freely if you see that you cannot make it. Don't hesitate. Be sure you are entering the seminary because you believe God wants you to do so."

There are six reasons why priests would discourage you from entering a seminary.

Motivation. First among all of these is the lack of proper motivation, according to 37 percent of the priests. One priest called it "a shallowness of motives."

None of the priests who mention motivation say exactly how they can detect a lack of proper motivation. Most of them added the word "attitude" indicating that a shallowness of motives probably comes out "in conversation or in a series of contacts over a period of time."

Generosity, conviction, balance, openness, love of people – these virtues, or the seeds of these virtues, are the basis of right motivation.

Education. The second reason for discouraging you would be your studies. If you have been a C to a D student in grade school and high school, chances are you will be discouraged by a priest from entering the seminary. A priest in Salina, Kansas, expresses it very bluntly as follows:

"I discourage some young men because 1. they don't have the brains, 2. they have bad family background and 3. they have undesirable personality traits."

Maturity. The third reason priests might discourage you is a general immaturity. A priest in a small Wisconsin town says he discourages young men when "I don't believe they would be able to hold up under the pressures and frustrations that modern priests have to face."

A Jesuit priest who is a psychological counselor says he discourages young men when they "are not emotionally mature." Another Holy Ghost priest who teaches lists these factors for discouraging young men:

"Ineptitude; psychological and emotional problems which are of long standing, serious and unresolved; educational ineptitude; escape artistry, that is, trying to use the priesthood as a method for solving unresolved problems."

Personality. Personality defects is another reason why 18 percent of the priests discourage considering the priesthood as a career. These personality defects can run the gamut of human qualities. As one Franciscan puts it, he will discourage young men for "lack of flexibility or plain stubbornness."

Health. Poor health is a reason for eight percent in discouraging young people. They are referring here mainly to physical health, not mental and emotional health which is covered in the other categories.

Celibacy. About one out of twenty priests say you should not consider the priesthood as a career if you feel you can't make it as a celibate.

A Jesuit writes that he will discourage a young man if he has a "strong need for feminine marital companionship."

This does not mean that these five percent of the priests are saying that you should dislike girls before you consider the priesthood as a career. What they are saying is that your attachment to members of the opposite sex should be a normal one, but not so strong as to require a great amount of feminine companionship.

Some priests do not discourage anyone, such as the Benedictine college professor from Pennsylvania who writes, "I don't discourage anyone, but I am very blunt about what it takes intellectually, spiritually, emotionally, and physically."

A priest of the Congregation of the Most Precious Blood, who works in the slums of Chicago, writes that he "never discourages anyone, for God's grace works in places we least expect."

And a priest from Greenville, South Carolina, says that he does not feel competent to discourage any young man from considering the priesthood. "I see the seminary as formation of willing guys, not a gathering of those who have already decided firmly that this is their life. The officials in the seminary are expert counselors who will help the men we send."

The men they send must be expertly prepared for the challenges which will face them later. They are not the same challenges facing priests today as you will see in the next chapter.

DISCOURAGEMENT FROM ENTERING THE SEMINARY

LACK OF CORRECT MOTIVATION

37%

POOR IN STUDIES

19%

IMMATURITY

19%

8% POOR HEALTH, PHYSICAL & MENTAL

PERSONALITY DEFECTS

18%

5% ATTACHMENT TO GIRLS

This is the advice priest respondents give to young men they discourage from entering the seminary. Over a fourth give more than one reason, bringing the total to 108 percent.

Challenges Today And Tomorrow

In my opinion the biggest challenge facing priests today is:

— "Generosity, openness to values and people outside the Church and continuous learning of things relevant to contemporary problems."

— "A spirit of sacrifice."

— "Renewing the Church and making religion relevant to the world."

— "The need to have an open mind and not attach oneself to any preconceived positions."

The biggest challenge facing priests of tomorrow, those to be ordained in the next ten years will be:

— "The competitive stature and quality of parallel professions that operate in individual counselling and social movements."

—"A crisis of faith which is a real problem today."

— "Maintaining the continuity with those priests ordained before the Second Vatican Council and exercising patience so that we may all do God's work."

— "Coping with change."

— "A gradual decline in the respect that people have for the priesthood."

There are 191 more comments concerning what priests feel represent the major challenges to the priesthood for today and for those priests to be ordained within the next ten years.

Using key words and the general meaning of the comments, the *challenges for today's priests* conveniently fall into six categories. The first two categories represent "outward challenges" facing the priesthood as a profession and the remaining four groupings represent "inward challenges" to the priest as a professional man.

Relevance. The first major challenge, according to 28 percent of the priests, might be termed "making religion relevant in today's world." In

the words of one young Salesian priest who teaches in one of the many Don Bosco technical institutes, the major challenge facing priests today is "to live Christ's counsels in a way that is meaningful to the modern mind."

Faith. The second major challenge can be called the "maintenance of Catholic faith in a sense of spirituality among people." A Philadelphia priest who spends full time in a parish says he feels that the major challenge facing priests today is "a persistent, continuing effort to be constantly prayerful, meditative, and truly spiritual." He feels that a highly developed spiritual life in today's world is a great goal as well as a tremendous challenge. A small town Iowa pastor puts it more simply, that is: "To be learned about the world and humble at the same time."

Obligations. The third major challenge facing priests now is the idea of remaining true to one-self with all the obligations of the priesthood. Some 22 percent mention a personal obligation including the vow of celibacy. Here are some expressions of this kind:

"Young priests who lack experience and are too progressive for the Church represent the biggest challenge facing the priesthood today," writes an older priest from Pittsburgh who was ordained over 25 years ago.

A younger priest from St. Louis states this personal challenge differently. He writes, "The biggest challenge facing a priest today is equipping himself for intelligent, competent, and interpersonal and social organizational work, rather than letting existing attitudes and institutional patterns carry him along." Another young priest who had just celebrated his 30th birthday says he feels that it is a big challenge to avoid the "comfort of the priesthood." He comes from a large parish

TODAY'S CHALLENGES

MAKING RELIGION RELEVANT IN TODAY'S WORLD	**28%**
MAINTAINING FAITH AND SPIRITUALITY	**26%**
REMAINING TRUE TO ONESELF WITH THE OBLIGATIONS OF THE PRIESTHOOD*	**22%**
OBEYING THE AUTHORITY OF THE CHURCH AS ORGANIZED	**17%**
FRUSTRATION AND UNCERTAINTY	**12%**
MEETING THE CHALLENGE OF VATICAN II	**10%**

This represents the opinion of 200 priests concerning what they feel are the biggest challenges facing them today. Some offer more than one challenge, bringing the total to 115 percent.

* About a third of these mention vow of celibacy.

where the living, if not "easy," presents few difficulties.

One-third of this group mentioned that the vow of celibacy presents a major challenge to their priesthood. Since this is a popular topic which has received much recent publicity, some in-depth interviews were conducted and the results are covered separately in the next chapter.

Obedience. The authority of the Church as it is presently organized presents the greatest challenge to about one out of six priests today. A priest from the Diocese of Cleveland notes that priests have a tremendous task to do, but this work, he feels, "must be done within the integrated and frustrating structures — and strictures — which encumber the Church in America."

Another priest in Yakima, Washington, feels that the greatest challenge facing priests today concerns the bishop and "having to recognize that the authority of the Church really rests with him."

The expressions of the priests in this category also deal with living in the rectory system with other priests who perhaps do not have the same interests and personality. It also contains comments from older priests who complain about the younger priests and comments from younger priests who feel that there are too many limitations on their "priestly zeal" and enthusiasm.

Change. Frustration and uncertainty represent a major challenge for one out of eight priests. According to one pastor in a small town Iowa parish, the biggest challenges facing priests today are the changes in the Church and the unrest among certain priests. Another in East Orange, New Jersey, who counsels college students feels that the changes are creating a confusion of the identity of the priest as a man and his identity in the role of a priest. He writes, "Many priests are not certain just who they are. Rapid changes have upset them, especially if they have been educated as most were in the somewhat rigid system of pre-Vatican Council II seminaries." This kind of uncertainty among priests, according to one in Fort Lauderdale, Florida, is expressed in his "trying to find the mind of the Church."

But all this change and uncertainty can be shaped to advantage, according to a 28-year-old Paulist priest in Chicago. He says that priests can work well within the Church's structures but reshape them so that the Church can intensify the relationship between God and man and man and his fellowman.

Vatican II. One out of ten priests mentions the results of Vatican Council II as the major challenge facing priests today.

The mission of the priest, because of the decisions of Vatican Council II which changed American Catholicism more rapidly than at any other period in its history, is more difficult to define. Vatican Council II raised numerous questions about the faith, the liturgy, the parish, relationships with other religions, war, poverty, racial discrimination and other issues of the day. Many priests mentioning the impact of Vatican Council II call it "an individual problem of interpretation." How each priest can make religion relevant in today's world and maintain faith and spirituality among his people are challenges of tremendous love and magnitude.

A seminary professor from Mundelein, Illinois, states, "Priests today face staggering problems. Celibacy and obedience are not the root problems. The real problem is that of priests' identity in a world that has side-stepped them and passed them by." He also noted priests live and work in a Church that is evolving and changing so rapidly, priests scarcely have time to catch their breath. "We feel like cogs in a great, impersonal juggernaut."

Vatican Council II and the whirlwind changes since have also been the source of challenges and some anxiety on the part of ministers of other faiths as well. The president of a Lutheran Synod reported recently that many Lutheran pastors are "frustrated" and "restless." The challenges of the day are not unique to the Catholic Church.

Tomorrow's Challenges. Today's priests have much advice to offer those who will be ordained during the next ten years. When all these comments are grouped, they seem to have the same headings as today's challenges, but the frequency

TOMORROW'S CHALLENGES

MAINTAINING FAITH AND SPIRITUALITY	**32%**
CONFORMITY AND AUTHORITY OF THE CHURCH	**25%**
COPING WITH CHANGE, WITH PATIENCE, PERSEVERANCE, DEDICATION	**20%**
MAKING RELIGION RELEVANT IN TOMORROW'S WORLD	**17%**
SAME AS THE CHALLENGES FACING TODAY'S PRIEST	**16%**
MEETING THE CHALLENGE OF VATICAN II	**7%**
CELIBACY	**4%**
DON'T KNOW	**4%**

The biggest challenge facing priests to be ordained in the next
ten years in the opinion of 200 priests are arranged according to frequency of
mention. Some offer more than one challenge, bringing the total to 125 percent.

of mentions gives each category a different emphasis. There are also six categories of challenges for the future priest but only one out of the six can be called an "outward challenge." All of the others are more or less personal challenges to the future priest himself.

Faith and Spirituality. The biggest challenge facing those priests to be ordained within the next ten years, according to one out of three of today's priests, will be the maintenance of faith and spirituality. In the words of one priest it will be "a willingness to sacrifice and to put the proper values on things that count for eternal salvation."

A 31-year-old Redemptorist, who spends most of his time studying and teaching, says that where today's challenge is "to be a man of faith in a world losing its faith," the biggest challenge facing the priest of tomorrow will be exactly the same only magnified. He writes, "In an age of sophistication priests of tomorrow will have to learn to pray and carry a cross to live the Gospel."

"I think it will be a crisis of faith which is already a real problem for many seminarians today. The present sense of insecurity and the disappearance of so many traditions and customs will call for stronger faith."

Obedience. The second major challenge facing priests of tomorrow, according to one out of four of today's priests, will be conformity to the authority of the Church. A pastor in a California mission church writes that priests of tomorrow must "be willing to accept the Church and its discipline." He feels that the direction some seminarians are receiving from young priests is a detriment to their vocations. He also writes that future priests must be prepared to work for change through the legitimately constituted authority of the Church.

Others see the problem of obedience eased through an effort to have all priests participate in decision making through diocesan senates, team apostolates and similar structures.

Change. Coping with change will be the third major challenge facing the priest of tomorrow, according to one out of five priests. They say that the old handy rules and regulations for doing a job will probably be gone and that the future must be looked forward to with patience, perseverance, and priestly dedication. A young Franciscan writes that the priest of tomorrow must be a more professional man but at the same time he will need to restrain his professional enthusiasm according to his own individual circumstances.

Relevance. One out of six of today's priests feels that the major challenge for the future will be making religion relevant in tomorrow's world. The same number, about 16 percent, feels that tomorrow's priests will face the same set of challenges as those facing the priests of today.

In comparing the two lists of challenges, the number one challenge facing priests today, according to the frequency of mentions, falls down to fourth place in the list of tomorrow's challenges. The faith-and-spirituality challenge, second on the list of today's challenges, is number one on the list of challenges facing the priests to be ordained in the next ten years.

The authority-of-the-church challenge, ranked as number four on the list for today, jumps up to the number two spot on the list of challenges facing tomorrow's priests. The uncertainty-challenge, number five on the list for today, jumps up to number three on the list of challenges for tomorrow.

Specific mentions of the implications and challenges of Vatican Council II rank fairly low today or tomorrow. Yet most of the challenges reveal the influence of Vatican Council II.

Since the vow of celibacy was mentioned by many of the priests in the survey and since this subject is receiving unprecedented publicity and attention, in-depth interviews were conducted to discuss this topic. The survey questionnaire sent to every priest did not specifically ask for comments about celibacy, yet over ten percent of the priests in the survey mention this somewhere in their questionnaire.

What is the controversy about priestly celibacy? The priests of today offer some insight into this question in the next chapter.

HOW CHALLENGES
CHANGE

RANK*	TODAY	TOMORROW (in the next ten years)
1.	Making religion relevant in today's world	Maintaining Catholic Faith and spirituality
2.	Maintaining Catholic Faith and spirituality	Conformity and obeying the authority of the church
3.	Remaining true to oneself with obligations and vows, including celibacy	Coping with "change," with patience, perseverance and dedication
4.	Obeying the authority of the Church as organized	Making religion relevant in tomorrow's world
5.	Frustration and uncertainty	Meeting challenges of Vatican II
6.	Meeting challenges of Vatican II	Celibacy
7.	Don't Know	Don't Know

16 percent of the respondents feel that challenges to priests will not change.

* By frequency of mention

Celibacy And Love

One of the three celibacy interviews takes place in a diocesan newspaper editor's office. The place looks like any editor's office: papers all about, books on the floor and on the desk a stack of mail yet to be opened. The priest-editor reports that he gets at least one story a week on the subject of celibacy.

The second interview takes place behind the stage of an auditorium at the University of Dayton. The priest being interviewed has just finished a talk to a summer mission institute and half of his audience consisted of sisters from many religious orders who are about to embark on an overseas mission in Africa or Southeast Asia. His talk, just delivered, has been well received and many priests, brothers, and sisters are attempting to continue the conversation on the subject of celibacy with this Marianist priest who has presented the subject of priestly celibacy in a frank and understanding way.

The third interview is conducted in the room of a priest who spends most of his time in the academic world as a college professor. He teaches theology to lay students as well as to major seminarians. The following represents their views on this timely subject:

What has been the Church's stand on celibacy?
Celibacy has long been considered as "an advantageous condition for priests." The positive benefits of celibacy for all priests were confirmed by some local councils in the Church as early as the 4th century even though it was not widely practiced until many centuries later.

The Church has always recognized that celibacy is a difficult way of life. Pope John XXIII is reported to have said on one occasion:

"Would you like to know what distresses me most? I do not mean as a man, but as Pope? The thought of those young priests who bear so bravely the burden of ecclesiastical celibacy causes me constant suffering. For some of them it is a martyrdom, yes, a kind of martyrdom. It often seems to me as if I were hearing a kind of plea — I do not mean right here, but from a distance — as if voices were demanding that the Church free them from this burden."

Pope Pius XII, in his 1950 letter on the priesthood, had stated the difficulty of celibacy in very clear terms. Paul VI admitted the tremendous burdens that celibacy places on the priest today in the June 24, 1967 Encyclical called "Priestly Celibacy."

Does celibacy cast priests in a dual role?

The conflict seems to lie in a difference of roles in which the priest, as a man, finds himself. On one hand he assumes a role of acting in God's place. On the other hand, society — concerned Catholic lay people — demand a different role of the priest. They want to deal with a priest as a man, as his true self.

Professional actors have the same problem when they throw themselves into a character role. Everybody sees the actor through a role, and that is why we often wonder what this actor is really like in true life. We understand the popularity of the "true" screen magazines which inform the public of what actors are "really" like.

Priests do not necessarily assume a character role like the actor. However, the priest is trained to assume what has become a very well defined role in the priesthood. For example, in the confessional, he can forgive in his role as a priest without forgiving from his true self. As another example, he can preach the spirit of poverty in his role of a priest and yet live in a comfortable rectory. He can preach charity yet find it difficult to be close to other people in personal relationships.

Can celibacy hinder maturity?

It seems that the greatest conflict about celibacy centers around the achievement of human values. Most of the objections to celibacy, according to one priest interviewed, "can be reduced basically to finding celibacy a hindrance to personal maturity and, consequently, to the ineffectiveness that results from the lack of human maturity." Therefore some priests seem to feel that

their celibacy has been a hindrance in their personal relationships.

The need of many people today is to have a priest relate to them on a person-to-person basis rather than through the role of yesterday. This places a real demand upon the priest to become first a real person.

What are some of the personal dangers of celibacy?

Celibacy can be a great insulation, enabling the priest to withdraw and isolate himself from others. For some it can lead to selfishness, especially what is referred to as the "selfish bachelor syndrome." For others, celibacy can lead to subtle forms of arrogance. When celibacy becomes an assumed role, a matter of personal detachment from the people a priest should serve, it loses its real value.

What are some of the personal advantages of celibacy?

Celibacy offers a singleness of purpose to the career of a priest. It creates the freedom to do the demanding work without the added responsibilities of raising a family. The reluctance of a wife to have her husband travel or relocate to another city has kept many corporation executives from advancing in their careers. The celibate is free to go all the way with his career with ample time for prayer, research and study in those fields which he thinks will help him do a better job. That takes lifetime dedication and celibacy can only help strengthen it. Other advantages are mentioned in the following paragraphs.

How would you describe celibate love?

First, celibate love is never exclusive in the sense that it is closed off to others. The celibate never offers himself to another or expresses his love to another in a way that automatically limits itself to one person alone. In contrast, the love in marriage, by its very nature, must be exclusive in its expression. The expression of sexual love is the most obvious area of exclusiveness. The beauty of sexual love lies in its exclusiveness. The beauty of celibate love lies not in its exclusiveness, but in its universal openness. It is in this sense that celibacy witnesses for the Christian to that future life with God the Father, Son and Holy Spirit where there will be neither marrying nor unmarrying.

The true celibate never limits his love to a given individual by anything which would bind him to restrain himself in a love relationship with another person. The true celibate remains free to develop any personal relationship completely because he has not limited himself to any area by an expression of exclusive loyalty.

Does celibate love create more freedom?

Yes, true celibate love allows what might be called a tremendous freedom of response. The celibate has no particular demand for responding to expressions of others who love him. The celibate wants the loved ones to feel no obligation at all toward him. The response of the loved ones is accepted by the celibate with gratitude because it is given freely. The loved ones also know that the celibate will never refuse to respond to love no matter what that response might be. This means that the celibate priest never expects a specific kind of response just because he is a priest and he never demands that others respond to him in his role as a priest.

What is the risk of celibate love?

Celibate love demands great maturity, because of the lack of confidence in it on the part of many.

"To leave a gift of self to many others unprotected demands a maturity and ability to withstand the hurt that comes from being taken advantage of," warns the Marianist priest.

Another risk of celibate love is that it carries a commitment to serving the needs of others and offering oneself to others for whatever good it will do them. It is obvious that the celibate cannot serve the needs of everyone at the same time. There are given instances when he does have to choose and every choice costs him. But the mature celibate recognizes his limitations and simply offers to others what he can and at the time and under the circumstances that he can do it. He must be content to offer whatever he has openly to anyone who wants it.

The third risk of celibacy is the fact that it is only meaningful in a relationship. Most celibates have been told in the past to remain celibate by avoiding relationships. Too often in the past they have never learned how to be "non-exclusive" in their relationships because they were not to relate at all. When priestly celibacy has the orientation of mature, human love, it is truly "a brilliant jewel."

Most people know priests only from a few moments' contact on Sunday mornings and by listening to them from the pulpit. Between Sundays, as you will see next, priests live a varied, professional and interesting life.

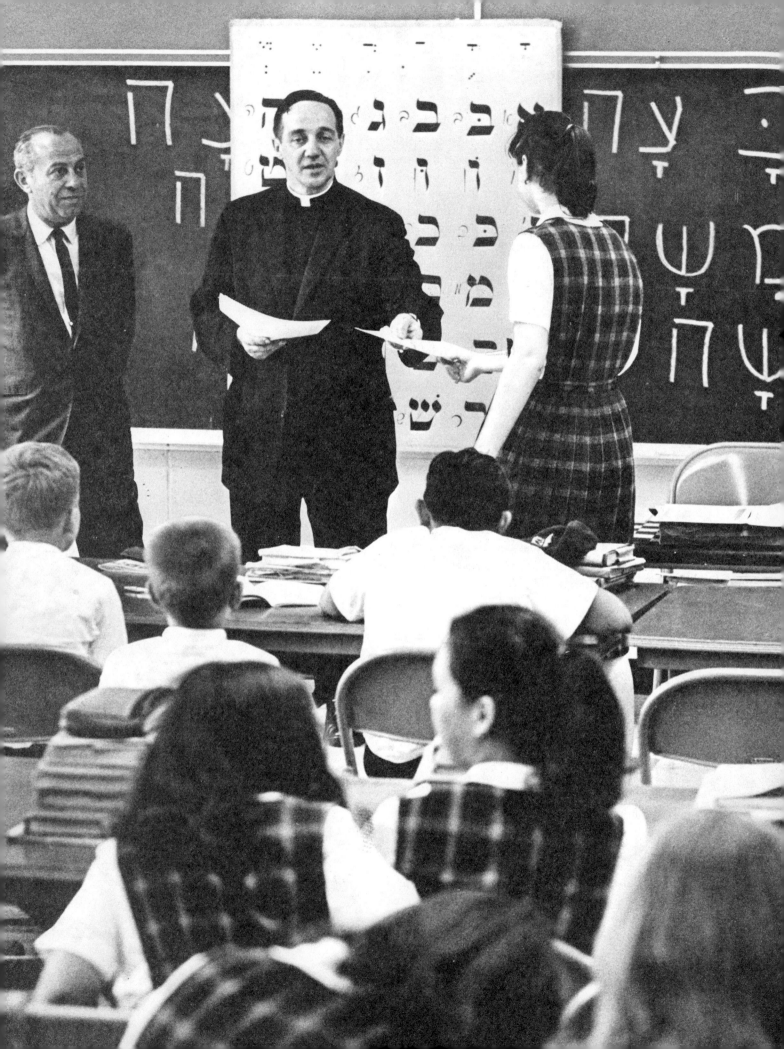

Between Sundays

On a rainy Wednesday a man walks down one of the narrow streets of inner Baltimore. He has six appointments to keep. He is on his way to the first.

In the afternoon he has a meeting with the city interracial council and as he walks past the marble steps of this Baltimore street he collects his thoughts. What he has to say this afternoon may help many people in his chosen world.

His world is a five-square-mile area in the middle of the city. In this world there are a thousand marble door steps and six thousand Negro families which he has defended many times and for which he was thrown in jail twice.

This man is a priest whose world used to be Philosophy at Louvain in Belgium and Theology at the American College in Rome. Father is now a fulltime parish curate and loves it.

✻   ✻   ✻

The door opens to a cheerful room in the Bronx and a pleasant, easy-going man extends his hand in greeting. The room is nicely furnished, with oil paintings on the wall. The chairs are very comfortable and an ash tray awaits lighting-up time.

This easy-going man is a counselling psychologist who opens that door several times a day. Some of the people who walk through have emotional problems of one kind or another. Some are what are called *schizoid* and *paranoid*. Some are alcoholics. He specializes in the treatment of alcoholics and is licensed to practice under the laws of the State.

He is a priest who describes his weekday career as "trying to get people to rejoin the human enterprise."

✻   ✻   ✻

On opening day, Monday, a professor faces his class of fifteen students at St. Thomas College in St. Paul.

"The purpose of this course, gentlemen, is to examine the phenological, morphological, lexical and syntactical aspects of the modern English language."

The course is English 409 for selected seniors

majoring in English. The professor is a specialist in the development of the English language and has five years teaching experience. He is working on his doctorate in linguistics at the University of Minnesota where he got his masters in 1961.

The professor happens to be a priest. He was ordained in 1958.

* * *

The phone rings in a parish rectory in a Pittsburgh suburb. It is 11:30 at night.

"Hello, hello, Father?" a scared, hesitating voice of a young woman inquires.

The parish assistant assigned to answering night calls reaches for the light switch. This sounds urgent. "Yes, Janet," he responds. "I recognize your voice."

"Father, I am calling from a pay phone. I've just been in an accident and my friends look hurt bad."

The priest gets the location and assures Janet he'll get there as soon as possible. He gets dressed fast and heads out, stuffing a little purple stole in his pocket. He cautions himself not to put too much of a heavy foot on the accelerator as he times his speed with the traffic lights.

At the scene he sees a familiar sight, two cars wrinkled out of shape with doors jarred open. The police lights twirl red flashes on three injured teenagers wrapped in blankets, lying on a glass-strewn pavement. Janet paces unsteadily nearby.

These young people are recognized by the priest. They are members of a parish club he moderates. He is happy Janet called him; she might not have for any number of reasons. She called her parish priest anyway.

This priest is available to young people. His parish programs for them have an underlying motive — to let people in his parish know he cares, to be approachable and available in a time of need.

Two of the young people on the pavement need a lot of help. They are seriously hurt and wait for an ambulance in a state of semi-consciousness. When they open their eyes they see the familiar, encouraging face of the priest. They don't hear what he is saying but they are glad to see him. They smile weakly to let him know.

This priest considered many careers before he entered the seminary. He was always interested in youth work and seriously thought of coaching and social case work as possible careers. A career as juvenile court counselor was another possibility that interested him.

Actually this parish priest became all three. He has taken special training before and since ordination which qualifies him for any of the careers he previously considered.

He doesn't like the gruesome scene of an auto accident any more than the next person, but he is happy he was called whatever the hour. He is also glad he could offer a little help.

After all, who calls up the coach or social worker at 11:30 at night when they are in trouble? They call a priest.

These are only a few examples of what priests do between Sundays and they represent how most priests spend their time when laymen are about their business of living and making a living from Monday through Friday. Priests are busy men in the community and that may mean the neighborhood community, national or world communities.

The parish is the most important of the many ways priests use to reach people. Slightly over a third of the priests spend a major portion of their time in pastoral activities similar to that of the priest in Baltimore. Yet this priest is typical of only a part of this group — one out of three priests — who are really active pastoral workers during the week. He is typical because he is actively IN with both feet — in his neighborhood visiting, observing, questioning, and as much as he can, improving.

There are others who find parish work interesting and challenging. Here are a few examples:

In a parish in Miami, Florida, a diocesan priest has spent his weekdays during the past five years with Cubans and established Cursillo programs with many of the neighborhood groups. He has learned Spanish and has promoted some difficult parish renewals with some pretty down-hearted refugees from Cuba. The challenge paid off.

In Catholic Boston one might think it is easy to be a parish priest. A Yankee New England priest spends his weekdays planning how to get things

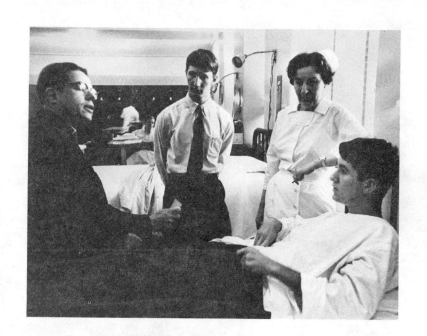

WEEKDAY OCCUPATIONS

63%	RELIGIOUS TEACHING AND FORMATION
37%	OTHER PARISH WORK
30%	OFFICE, INCLUDING PARISH ADMINISTRATION
27%	COUNSELLING
11%	OTHER
8%	HOSPITAL WORK
7%	STUDY
6%	WRITING

Three out of four priests have more than one of the above occupations, bringing the total to 178 percent.

done with and through his parishioners. He plans suggestions and approaches to take with all parish organizations. He knows that to create a Christian community everyone must work together.

In pleasant Yakima, Washington, it's the same way for parish priests. They probably work a little differently from those in Boston. One priest says he is out there in the neighborhood all week long — with the people.

A few priests are not so lucky as to see the opportunities in parish work or it may be that they don't have the chance to exercise them. A priest in Louisville, Kentucky, says most of his weekday time is taken up with uninteresting tasks. Another in a sleepy Louisiana town writes that most of his weekdays are taken up with relaxation.

Most parish priests find the telephone a favorite pastoral tool. People with all kinds of needs call at every hour of the day and night. A young priest in Buffalo, ordained over two years, calls this service "watching the house." The ringing telephone is the response of people to the available priest.

With about 60,000 priests in the country, some 37 percent devote full time to parish work outside of formal teaching. Some are good at it. Some are happy at it and in their own opinion less than one out of twelve are dissatisfied with their parish duties, contrary to publicity in the newspapers.

Parish work is challenging. Seminaries recognize this now and place more emphasis on what they call "pastoral theology." Parish work is an organization and planning job in many respects. It is also leadership, a feeling for people, an active rather than a contemplative life. There is a lot of diplomacy and public relations required in parish work, especially now and during the next ten years when the parish is expected to change a great deal.

According to the survey, the biggest single occupation during the week for priests, however, is either full or part-time teaching. About four out of ten priests today have a piece of chalk in their hands sometime between Sundays. It is not necessarily the job for advanced learning as the example of the college professor implied. Priest teachers are lecturing on almost any subject in grade school, high school and college. It is a great way to iden-

tify with people, especially younger people.

In Eau Claire, Wisconsin, for example, a parish priest teaches a grade at Sacred Heart School. In the small town of Hankinson, North Dakota, a curate teaches both in grade school and high school. Another example of a real schedule is a priest of Cincinnati, Ohio, who teaches 25 classes per week in high school.

Some priests are close to teaching by working in Newman student centers, such as the chaplain at the University of Nebraska at Lincoln. Another in Akron, Ohio, combines teaching with sociological research.

In the ecumenical age more priests teach in state universities and are on the faculties of religion or philosophy departments.

About half of the teaching group are religion instructors at all levels. Most priests mention that they have "catechetics" in grade school. Many report that they give special instructions for converts or prospective brides and grooms. A priest in Arizona plans religious training programs for the whole diocese through the C.C.D. program and he says he spends about 60 percent of his weekday time on that alone. Religious teaching goes to the top with theology in seminaries — teaching future priests. One of the Missionaries of the Sacred Heart in Shelby, Ohio, is a good example of that and on weekends he is in a parish like most priests. A Holy Ghost Father from Norwalk, Connecticut, is another example. He teaches pastoral theology during the week and then helps out by saying the 10:30 and 12:00 Masses on Sunday in a nearby parish.

Another priest, a Salesian of Ramsey, New Jersey, teaches in the Don Bosco High School there. He says his school has turned out over a hundred priests in its fifty year history. That averages two a year and one of them became a bishop.

About three out of ten priests in the United States are involved in office work as one of their major duties during the week. One priest is principal of Bishop Timon High School in Buffalo, New York, and is in charge of 13 lay teachers, 27 priest teachers and 1,011 students at last count. That means a lot of paper work.

The office jobs that priests fill from Monday

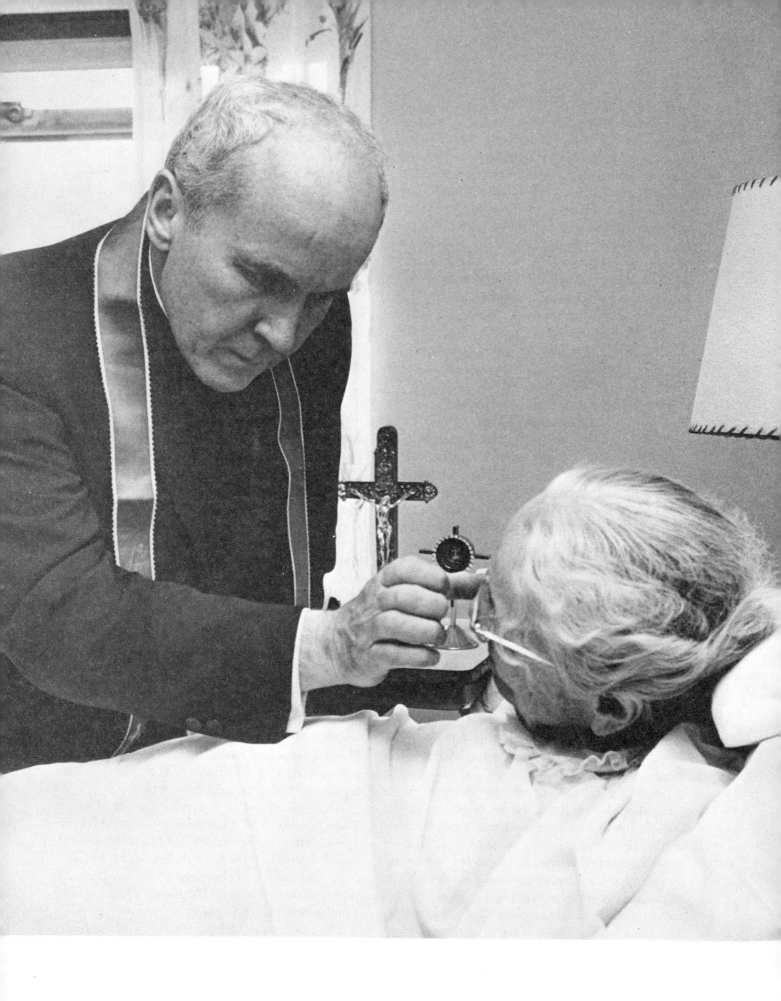

through Friday are about as varied as the many professional positions. A young priest works in the diocesan chancery office at Seattle, Washington, and an even younger Benedictine runs a monastery outside Canon City, Colorado. With 90 Benedictines in the place he finds himself in the office most of the time. There are others — architects, engineers, lawyers, scientists, etc.

Counselling is another important weekday occupation and 27 percent of the priests are likely to be counselors. This includes marriage counselling and spiritual counselling of one kind or another, but most do psychological counselling. Many priests have their own practices as counselling psychologists.

A priest at Duquesne University in Pittsburgh, teaches and maintains a private counselling practice. With his extra time he is a juvenile court chaplain.

Much of the counselling is guidance work in high schools and colleges. Many priests study for professional degrees in psychology to get them into this type of work or they often decide to learn more about it after they find they have been assigned to counselling. Almost one of three young priests today do get this type of assignment.

Hospital work of any kind, in most cases being a chaplain, is a weekday occupation for eight percent of the priests. A Kansas City, Missouri, priest is a chaplain in a state mental hospital. A Kalamazoo, Michigan, priest is involved in mental therapy. With about a thousand Catholic hospitals, 387 homes for the aged and 257 orphanages in the United States, at least that many priests are needed during the week to take care of their religious requirements.

About seven percent of the priests study during the week. They have an additional professional goal in administration, psychology, teaching, or some other field that requires their full time at least for a few years. About half the priests say that chances for advancing one's education after the seminary are good.

About one out of sixteen priests in the country write. They edit some 120 Catholic newspapers and many of these with laymen. About 90 dioceses in the country have a public relations priest to handle requests for information from newspapers, TV and radio. More are involved in writing and editing for magazines. Also in this category are the good old-fashioned preachers. Today they are experimenting with new kinds of parish renewal programs, retreats, missions and other means of turning men's hearts to God.

The priest in the sleepy Louisiana town who "relaxes all week" is one in a thousand. The average priest today and certainly tomorrow is and will be a busy, busy man.

Priests, brothers and sisters find that one of the most active fields today and tomorrow is and will be social action as you will see in the next chapter.

Relevance Of Action

One interview on social action is held in the inner part of a midwestern city. The place is a storefront Montessori school for youngsters in the area who have little chance to break out of the poverty barrier as they grow older. The sister-teacher running this school says that her deep involvement in social action through specialized education is the basis of her vocation and its greatest reward.

A second interview on social action takes place in a trailer-house which doubles as a chapel. It is mid-July in Michigan and a young, Spanish-speaking priest from south Texas talks about his work among migrant workers who have worked their way up with the harvest. This priest is for all practical purposes the pastor of a travelling parish that will dissolve in the fall and regroup the next spring when the migration starts again.

A third interview on social action happens on the front porch of an Appalachian rectory which used to belong to a family who moved to Chicago in search of greater opportunity, namely, any kind of a job. The priest lives in this ramshackle house to get closer to the people he is trying to help.

He is young, bright-eyed and from upstate New York, but not naive about the big job to be done. He has a degree in sociology and knows a lot about ways to help but is aware it will take a lot more than that to offer new hope and direction for most of his people.

The following represents a combination of the views of a sister and two priests on a subject which seems to motivate most who seek a professional career in the religious life:

What is social action?
Social action generally refers to the programs carried on in the United States by priests, brothers and sisters. These programs first got their start under the banner of "home missions" contrasting them to mission activities in foreign countries. Today *social action* means a program of some kind which is set up to help people improve the situations in which they find themselves — *helping people to help themselves*. Conversion and catechetics take a secondary position in these programs, although religion is obviously an important part of all social action.

8

What are the different kinds of social action?

There are "inner city" programs that assist those who live in slums. These programs can deal with education, urban renewal, health, housing, any number of problems depending upon the city and the needs of the people.

Teaching has always been a social action program and the educational field is increasing in its importance in all aspects. All social action or helping programs are educational to some degree. They include not only the regular grade school and high school, but the trade schools, youth programs of all kinds, schools for exceptional children and many others. Social action is a big, big field and the opportunities for selecting a career specialty within its confines are almost unlimited.

Who are social action programs for?

Most social action programs are aimed at poor people — those single people who must support themselves on $30 a week or less, married couples who make $38 a week or less, families of three who take in $47 a week or less and families of four who are paid $60 a week or less. There are 35 million Americans in this category and the socially-active priests, brothers and sisters are working with them in professional, planned programs. Most of these people are white — 24.5 million of them — or one out of seven white Americans. The non-white poor are mostly Negroes — 10.5 million — or one out of every two non-white Americans.

Where are social action programs operating?

Half of them operate in the cities and half somewhere in Appalachia and the South. It is estimated that 9.3 million families exist on less than $60 a week income. Five million of them live in cities and 4.3 million live in Appalachia and the South. These are the people who have been forgotten by progress, unchanged by government welfare programs and unaffected by the employment opportunities brought on by the business boom.

What created the need for social action in cities?

In the 1940's over seven million people moved from the urban areas into suburbs, deserting the central parts of the cities. The changing picture in employment which followed soon thereafter left vast numbers of people who did not move to the suburbs stranded without opportunities. Chicago's South Side, for example, lost industries within a five-year period which employed 50,000 workers supporting nearly half a million people. This pattern repeated itself in many other cities across the country.

What is the role of priests and sisters in social action?

They provide part of the professional cadre who fight and guide others in waging war on poverty. Social action requires more than dispensing money or goods to the poor, a lot more. Priests and sisters trained in sociology, education, psychology and a number of other fields often establish, or help to set up complex programs that combine the resources of government and private foundations with their deeply-rooted awareness of social justice and the hopes of the poor to help themselves. This means that many priests and sisters (and dedicated laymen active in these programs) actually live in the areas and neighborhoods of the people they are serving. It means that they live and work under conditions foreign to anything they might have experienced growing up in the average middle-income family.

Does the government help these people?

Yes, the government has many programs on the city, state and federal level. But the government cannot do it alone even if it had the qualified people to give these programs a "personal touch" which it does not. A Mayor in a leading eastern city says, "You have to have earthly people willing to take on the dirty work." Priests, brothers and sisters make up a significant part of the corps of specialists who are doing the tough, front-line action in the nation's war on poverty.

What are priests and sisters doing, for example?

In the migrant areas there are over two million Mexicans, Negroes, Puerto Ricans and whites with their children who roam the country, working in the fields for substandard wages. Because of a language barrier in most cases and the brief time they are in any community these migrant families have little opportunity to benefit from the communities they live in. Priests and sisters organize tutoring groups of high school students and adults who go out to the migrant camps to teach. They set up summer schools, scouting programs, recreational programs, night English-Spanish classes for the workers and day care centers for migrant worker children. They do as much as they can to make the migrant families welcome as long as they are in the community. There are a few cases of priests travelling with migrant troups, ministering to their temporary parishes from a house trailer chapel.

Is teaching a social action career for those in religious life?

Definitely, since its main concern is human growth and understanding. The greatest activity of priests, brothers and sisters combined is teaching, according to the survey, and this type of social action extends beyond the poor, even beyond the familiar role they have in parish schools, Catholic high schools and colleges. Instructing the poor on practical, non-religious matters provides some of the most dramatic examples of a teaching career. Yet other priests, brothers and sisters fulfill a social action mission when they conduct a seminar on modern business practices, lecture as visiting professors at a state university, conduct an experimental youth program, or deliver a television series on child psychology for parents. This emphasis on social action in an apparent non-religious context by no means compromises or minimizes the role of these teachers, even if they are priests, brothers or sisters. On the contrary, they have tremendous jobs on their hands to bring a Christian theological orientation to a particular segment of our society, whether that be the poor, youth or middle-class suburbanite.

In this chapter brief mentions are made of the contributions brothers make in the field of social action. A separate survey reveals a professional profile of over a dozen communities and is reported in the next chapter.

Brothers' Report

There are about 13,000 men in the United States who chose to live a religious community life and pursue a career which suits their individual interests. This report contains the responses of one hundred brothers who feel their lives and problems are somewhat uncomplicated.

What interested these men most in becoming a brother is natural and unanimous. Everyone indicates that his major influence in choosing this kind of life was the contact with brothers each had during school years. The example of the brothers who taught them in grade school or high school is mentioned by every brother who responded to the survey. A few mention an additional thought, such as the desire to live a community life or love for the Church and its teachings.

As one student brother with the Marianists put it, "It was the real togetherness or family spirit of the brothers when I was in high school. They showed me great respect and attention as a person."

Writes another brother who took his final vows 13 years ago, "I knew some dynamic brothers who would listen to my adolescent tensions, who would play in our dance band practice and one afternoon called to see if I had gotten rid of the flu."

Who Brothers Are. Brothers are mostly professional men; they are not the pots-and-pans specialists for religious institutions. Over 86 percent of the brothers in the survey have college degrees; 80 percent of these got their degrees after entering the religious life. Those who do not have a degree number only 14 percent and some of these have associate certificates in applied mechanics or have completed formal training in a variety of trades.

The respondents are mostly young men. Three out of four are 35 years of age or younger. Here

is a breakdown of the age group of the brothers surveyed:

Students in their late teens or early twenties	19%
Graduate brothers 21-30	40%
31-40	25%
41-50	9%
51-60	6%
Over 60	1%
	100%

What Brothers Do. Most of the brothers are teachers. At least nine out of ten mention this as one of their principal professional occupations. The remainder have other interesting jobs. A 25-year-old Brother of St. Pius X, for example, is a graduate nurse and an inhalation therapy student. A 29-year-old Franciscan brother is a research biologist and a 25-year-old Alexian brother is a mechanical engineer. Other non-teaching occupations in the twenty to thirty age group include librarian, social worker, secretarial and administration work, retreat, vocation, and education program coordinators.

The occupations of brothers may indicate why certain men choose to become brothers rather than priests. Brothers, like priests, all have a general desire to serve their fellow human beings within the structure of Church organization. But brothers seem to have an idea of what they want to do with their careers and fit their desire to be a teacher, engineer, etc., into the brotherhood. Combined with a desire to serve in the Church, they feel that both desires can be satisfied in the brotherhood much more readily.

A young 27-year-old Marianist who is a registered nurse says, "Young religious should not get a false sense of obedience and be forced to follow a special profession in which they may have no

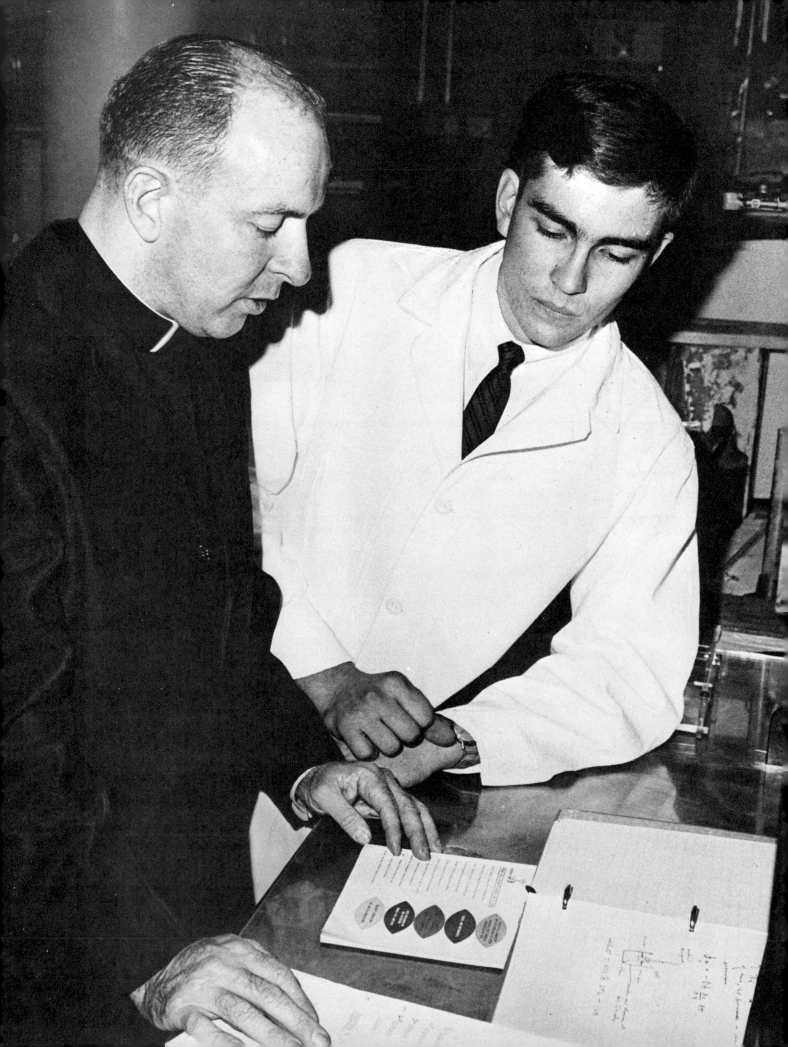

BROTHERS' VOCATION OBSTACLES

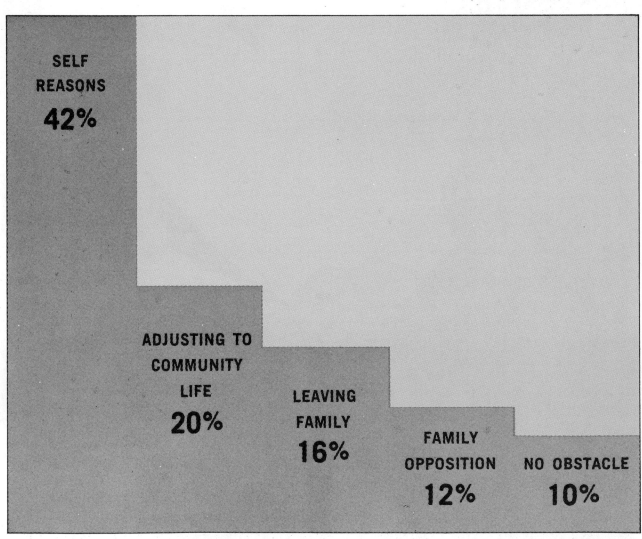

SELF
REASONS
42%

ADJUSTING TO
COMMUNITY
LIFE
20%

LEAVING
FAMILY
16%

FAMILY
OPPOSITION
12%

NO OBSTACLE
10%

interest or talent. Know *first* what you want to do. If you are not happy and cannot find fulfillment in a daily occupation, you certainly will not have that fulfillment made up for you in the brotherhood."

This is from a 50-year-old brother who has been in for 30 years. He writes, "I felt an attraction to teaching and school life. Besides, I joined an order of priests and brothers on the basis of equality, so I was playing it cool. The 'democracy' and modernity of the order at the time I joined appealed to me. Thank God my order kept up with the times."

Brotherhood and Priesthood compared. Almost four out of ten of the brothers state that they felt that their talents, abilities and interests led them to choose the brotherhood rather than the priesthood. In their opinion the seminary would not guarantee the desired profession or occupation after ordination. Other brothers mention that their evaluation of their own talents and abilities suited them better for a particular career. The scholastic education given in a seminary was not their cup of tea.

About three out of ten brothers compare their role as a brother with that of the priesthood. This group of men say that they feel their role as a person contributing to and serving others as a teacher or a nurse is what they themselves want to do. They feel they can relate better to others as an individual person with or without a priestly stole. This group of brothers also indicates that the role of priest has more of the function of being an intermediary between God and men through the liturgy and sacraments. Although this functional picture is changing in the priesthood, the basic role of the priest himself remains even if the Mass and sacraments take up so little of his time. Therefore almost three out of ten brothers indicate that they would rather work and serve the Church as a brother without the added responsibilities that are placed upon priests.

A Christian brother explains, "Basically I felt that the priesthood was not my vocation. Having a great regard for the dignity of the priest, I felt that I wanted to be a religious teacher, a brother who would be in contact with youth in every respect, in the classroom as well as outside of class."

The survey of the priests does indicate that priests are not in contact with young people perhaps as much as they could be. The influence of priests upon young people is not as marked as the priests themselves admit in their survey. Yet 100 percent of the brothers state they were plainly impressed by the warm personalities and kind interests of the brothers who had taught them.

In asking the brothers why they chose the brotherhood instead of the priesthood, two out of ten brothers simply state that they had no personal desire or feelings about the priesthood. A Brother of St. Pius X who is in his mid-twenties puts it this way, "I just honestly felt that I did not desire to become a priest. I had no inclinations along that line as I became older and more mature."

Another 14 percent of the brothers indicate, without comparing their vocation with the priesthood, that they had a simple, straightforward calling to the brotherhood. A young Marianist expresses the brotherhood as a complete calling in itself. He says, "I wanted to teach, guide, and work with youth directly and without the extra responsibility of the ministry."

Obstacles to the Brotherhood. Brothers mention a number of obstacles which may have temporarily blocked their decision to join a particular order. Better than four out of ten brothers give some "self" reason. About five out of ten brothers responding specifically mention the fact that they knew they were to forfeit female companionship, marriage, and the eventual establishment of a family. They also know they made this choice freely.

Other self reasons, rare instances, are lack of funds, poor health and scholastic standing.

About 20 percent of the brothers indicate that the adjustment to community life was an obstacle. About one third of this group indicates the rules and authority of a particular order which they joined. They feel that rules were archaic and the authorities over them were a bit hard to take. One brother mentions that his most difficult obstacle

ADVICE FROM
BROTHERS

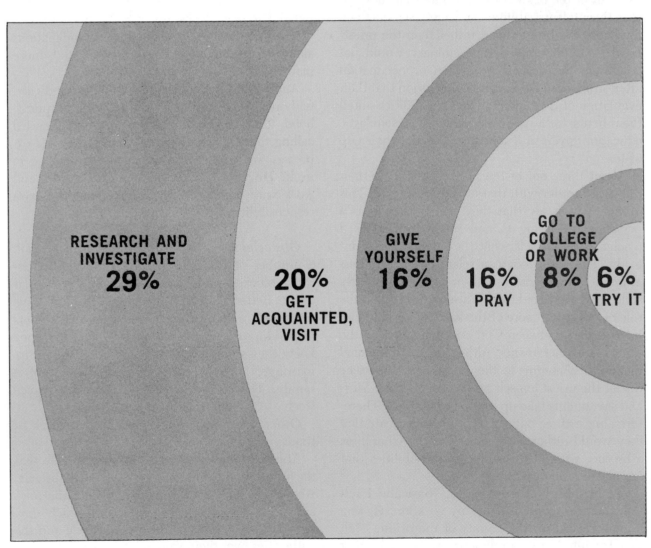

RESEARCH AND
INVESTIGATE
29%

20%
GET
ACQUAINTED,
VISIT

GIVE
YOURSELF
16%

16%
PRAY

GO TO
COLLEGE
OR WORK
8%

6%
TRY IT

was learning to accept the rules of the order quietly without questioning each and every one. He now recognizes this is a universal problem in any walk of life.

Leaving home and loved ones represented an obstacle for 16 percent of the brothers. Only one out of eight brothers mentions parental opposition as an obstacle to his vocation. This is about half of that for priests and nuns combined. One out of ten brothers is fortunate in that he did not feel that his vocation was blocked in any significant way. As one brother writes, "I do not believe I had any major obstacles in my decision to become a brother."

Advice from a Brother. Brothers tend to be practical and natural in their advice to young men who think they might have a calling to be a brother. Almost three out of ten brothers advise young men to investigate, research and study various religious orders that have brothers. Two out of ten brothers advise young men to get acquainted on a more personal basis with brothers in those communities which interest them.

Some suggest choosing a large and financially stable organization. Other brothers suggest that young men select one of the most up-to-date groups which have changed their constitution and rules to adapt to the post-Vatican II age.

A 29-year-old Franciscan brother writes, "The order of brothers that I joined is not the same to which I was originally attracted nor the order that taught me in school. I attribute this to the lack of personal relationship between the brothers I had in school and myself. I met the Franciscan brothers accidentally and I was immediately taken by their very warm and personal manner."

Another 16 percent give spiritual advice of one kind or another. This includes working with a spiritual director and having a regular prayer program which will help put any vocation into the proper perspective.

Many of the older brothers, and almost as many young brothers, advise a young man to go to college and work for a few years before entering. Eight percent of the brothers, evenly divided between young and old, offer this advice. They say,

"Don't enter before you finish high school at least."

Six percent just say go ahead and try it, quit if you don't like it. Five percent offer no advice. This group feels that advice to a young man ought to be personal and individual and that no good advice can be offered of a general nature.

A Franciscan brother, 29 years old, responding to the question concerning advice to young men, writes, "I really don't like this question. I don't think there is any universal advice to aspirants. They should certainly make their own decision and I think I would tell them to beware of following advice blindly."

In summing up, an elderly brother about to retire as a theology professor looks back and reflects, "The dominant motive that made sense for my religious life was to pursue a desire to teach while living primarily with God and in God. This was the greatest love fulfillment of my being."

Brothers seem to know what they want to do professionally before they enter religious life. The motivation of young women in selecting this life is quite different, as you will see in the next chapter.

Why She Became A Sister

It is only rarely that most of us are able to ask a sister directly why she chose life in a convent. Yet, the written answers from sisters in parish convents all over the country show that the reasons are very simple and natural.

Example. Over half of the sisters responding to the survey, specifically 55 percent, say that it is the example of other sisters that influenced them most in their decision to enter the convent. This is only 11 percent more than the parallel reason that influences boys in considering the priesthood. Answer after answer in the survey repeated the words "example of a sister" in grade school or high school.

A Dominican Sister from a parish in St. Louis, Missouri, who now teaches grade school writes, "I believe the joy and happiness of the sisters whom I had in high school made me realize that the life of a religious was a happy one."

A Franciscan of Christian Charity who teaches in junior high school called it "the dedication of those in the field." A Sister of Mercy who teaches grade school in New Britain, Connecticut, writes, "The example given by the Sisters of Mercy who taught me in grammar school and high school influenced me most; their kindness, interest, approachability, and self-sacrifice for others helped me make my decision."

"What influenced me most in becoming a nun was contact with the sisters of the community. I finally entered. Genuine kindness in the classroom and their warm-hearted interest and unbounded joy which permeated their dealings with me made me see the beauty of a life dedicated to love." This is from a Sister of Mercy who teaches seventh grade in Hartford, Conn.

Spiritual. About 21 percent of the sisters in the survey say they entered the convent for spiritual reasons. This ranks number two on the list of reasons for sisters, whereas priests list this as num-

SISTER VOCATION
INFLUENCE

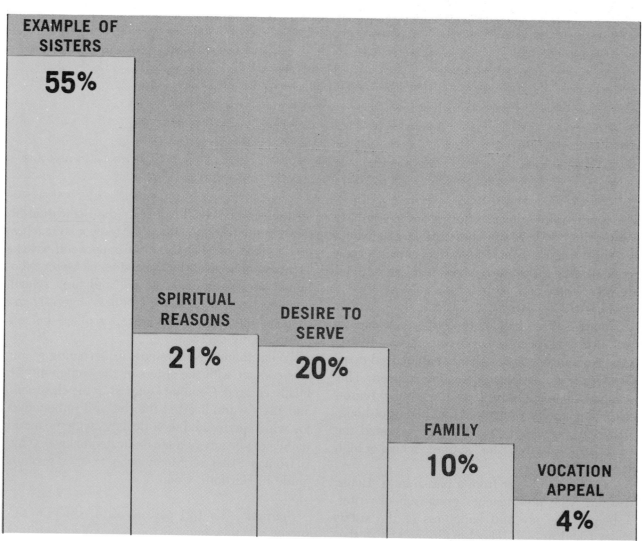

EXAMPLE OF SISTERS

55%

SPIRITUAL REASONS

21%

DESIRE TO SERVE

20%

FAMILY

10%

VOCATION APPEAL

4%

Of all the above influences named by 500 sisters, about one out of
ten stated more than one, bringing the total to 110 percent.

ber four in their reasons for entering a seminary. Many sisters give as their spiritual reasons "a love of Jesus."

Other spiritual reasons were expressed in various ways. One Sister of Mercy from Meriden, Connecticut, writes simply, "I wanted peace of soul." Another from Stamford, Connecticut, combines her observation of the example of her teachers and a spiritual reason — "the observation that nuns were happy, holy people who loved God above all and who showed this love by serving others."

A Franciscan Sister in Stamford, Connecticut, who took her final vows last year, writes this recollection of her childhood dreams:

"When I was in the fourth grade I wanted to be a sister just so I could write on the blackboard. In the fifth grade the reason switched to the fact that I liked walking in long dresses. In the sixth grade I had the idea my penmanship might improve if I became a sister. Our seventh grade sister loaded us up with homework and my motive changed again; I would be a nun who wouldn't give out homework.

"When I was in the eighth grade I was most impressed with the ceremony as my older sister received the Franciscan habit. These reasons all sound childish and indeed they are, but they kept alive a little spark through all the years that grew into a mature love for His service."

Many sisters expressed their spiritual reason in a manner similar to this School Sister of Notre Dame from West Allis, Wisconsin, "What influenced me most was a desire to give more to God than I would have been able to do had I remained in the world. Added to this I had unselfish, loving parents and a good education from dedicated religious."

Service. Ranking very close to spiritual reasons is a personal desire to serve, according to two out of five sisters. Where this ranks third in the list of reasons for sisters, it ranked second in the list of reasons for priests.

The desire to serve also was expressed in a variety of ways. A Sister of St. Joseph in Wheeling, West Virginia, says that her biggest influence was an appreciation of "the needs of other people who find it difficult, sometimes impossible, to find happiness and reality themselves."

Many of the respondents contributed their inspiration to enter the convent to their awareness of the need and their ability to serve in a mission field. An Irish Sister of Mercy in Ballwin, Missouri, recalls as her influence "a missionary sister who returned to spend a vacation with her parents in my home town." Although this helped her to decide to enter the convent, she did not become a missionary sister herself. Today she teaches in the same order of sisters that taught her in grammar school.

Another sister says she was also influenced by a desire to serve, particularly in the mission field, and she chose to become a Maryknoll Sister. What influenced her most, she writes, was "the mission ideals portrayed in the lives of great people and missionaries — the desire to help others." Today she is doing catechetical work at Maryknoll, New York, and is awaiting her first assignment overseas.

Family. Family background is mentioned as an influence on about ten percent of the sisters responding, compared with 18 percent of the priests. A Franciscan Sister in Chicago says simply that her biggest influence was "my good home and wonderful, generous parents."

A School Sister of St. Francis in Barrington, Illinois, writes that it was "a well grounded appreciation for deep spiritual values and application of faith instilled in me by my mother." And another teaching Sister of Mercy from Independence, Missouri, states that it was "my mother's attitude toward religion and religious commitment."

Vocation Appeal. A few sisters say they simply don't know why they entered the convent nor can they remember what influenced them most. But, about four percent admit that they reacted to a convincing vocation appeal on the part of another sister or priest. One of the answers in this category comes from a Sister of Notre Dame De Namur who teaches fifth grade in Kettering, Ohio. She writes that her greatest influence in entering the convent was "a sermon in which our assistant pastor stated emphatically, 'I firmly believe that one out of every large family has a religious vocation.' It struck like lightning. Our family consisted of seven children. The others were all married. I was the only one left."

A radio broadcast on "Love and Marriage" had an opposite effect on a Notre Dame Sister who teaches in New York City. After hearing these thoughts, she writes, she decided to enter the convent.

Of the approximately 500 sisters who participated in the survey, 90 percent took their final vows less than ten years ago. About 42 of the sisters took their final vows four years ago or less.

According to the sisters themselves, 63.6 percent take their final vows between the ages of 23 and 26. Some 21.5 percent take their final vows between the ages of 27 and 30. Less than ten percent take their final vows between the ages of 18 and 22 and about one out of twenty enter late enough to receive their final vows between the ages of 31 and 45.

In the age bracket of 23 to 26, the popular age to take final vows is 25. One out of four sisters said she took her final vows at that age. Most of the sisters in this popular age bracket entered the convent after they had completed their high school education.

For many the attraction to the convent was offset by some real obstacles. For each type of "greatest attraction" just related there is a corresponding "greatest obstacle," as you will see next in the chapter on convent obstacles.

Convent Obstacles

The greatest obstacle in becoming a nun, they say, is the young woman herself, not her family, not her friends.

Self. Over 34 percent of the sisters responding say their own indecision, lack of confidence, spiritual independence and even a strong desire to marry and raise a family are among the "self" obstacles they had to face.

"Doubt as to whether I could really live what we promise God was my obstacle," recalls a second grade teacher from Des Moines, Iowa.

"I didn't think I was the 'nunny' type," writes another from Ft. Lauderdale, Florida. "But you know there isn't a 'nunny' type."

"Very definitely the greatest obstacle to my religious vocation was the interior battle with *self*," declares a Sister Servant of the Immaculate Heart of Mary. "No parental skepticism, no raised eyebrows, no fiance's dismay could ever prove as difficult to cope with as my own love of complete independence, my own interior repugnance at giving totally of myself."

"My own strong desire for a husband and children, the need of being made to feel wanted and loved was my biggest obstacle," confides a Sister of Charity BVM, who now works as a sacristan in a cathedral parish.

A professor who teaches psychology and education at a prominent Catholic college in Kansas writes that the biggest block in her vocation was "my love for the world and all that it implies." She explains further, "Separation from very close friends, family, giving up offers already proposed to continue my training in scientific research, sacrificing the intimacy and personal love of the family at home were all great blocks in the way of my vocation."

"After the novelty of religious life wore away, I found myself looking back to all that I had left behind. I had to learn to give all or nothing and this involved a great struggle. I almost left to return to what I had before," writes another Benedictine Sister who now teaches in a parish in a small Pennsylvania town.

A Sister of Charity who teaches at the cathedral

11

high school in Denver, Colorado, expresses it another way — "Accepting in a true Christian spirit many different personalities and temperaments of the sisters you live with."

Another high school teacher, a Franciscan Sister from Rochester, Minnesota, writes, "I was attracted to dedication, but wanted more freedom than that accorded to a sister." She was a college student when she entered, took her final vows at the age of 24 and now is very busy as a counsellor and youth group moderator in addition to her teaching duties.

Another self reason might be termed fear of the unknown. A Marian Sister in Waverly, Nebraska, confides, "I had almost no idea as to what was involved; I was afraid of the unknown."

Reflects a Sister of Providence from Fayetteville, North Carolina, "It seems to me to have been a fear of stepping into the unknown, perhaps a fear of failure due to excessive shyness and lack of self-confidence. Coupled with this, the novitiate was a 24-hour distance from home by train. When I look back, I know that only God's actual grace gave me the courage."

The unknown caused a School Sister of Notre Dame to think of sisters as "creatures to be admired from a distance." She called this her chief hindrance because of her fear and lack of knowledge of what sisters and convent life were really like.

Another self reason which the sisters themselves found to be an obstacle in their past decision to enter the convent was the adjustment to authority. Many sisters admit they found it difficult to adjust to the rules and regulations of convent life, many of which have been discontinued and now seem petty. A second grade Sister of St. Agnes who teaches in Muncie, Indiana, expresses it this way, "I am a person with a lot of initiative and found it hard to be suppressed by my superiors. Following a strict daily schedule even during postulancy was another obstacle. I couldn't understand why we all had to do the same thing at the same time. Too much uniformity. So frequently unity, which I thought was so necessary, was sadly lacking for the sake of uniformity."

"My fear of losing my identity as a person was my biggest hindrance. I did not begin to lose this fear until my freshman year of college when I met sisters who gave living evidence that this need not happen. Later I realized that we were not being formed in a mold but our community actually respects the individuality of each person." At the age of 25 this Sister of the Holy Humility of Mary is now teaching in a parish school at Painesville, Ohio.

There are other interesting self reasons why young women found it difficult to make a decision on a convent career. "In my opinion, as I look back now," writes a 30-year-old teacher from Warwick, Rhode Island, "I was much too young at 15 to cope with an adult life. Adolescence spent in a convent was torture. This was my greatest cross and I feel that the authorities should never have allowed me to enter so young."

Another obstacle is escape. A Sister from St. Paul, Minnesota, relates the biggest obstacle she had to face in becoming a nun was "suspicion that my vocation was an escape from the world which I felt inadequate to face."

There are other very human and touching obstacles, such as reported by the Sister of St. Joseph of Carondelet, who now teaches in a parish school at Waco, Texas. Here is her story:

"I found it hard to get used to living with girls from a different part of the United States. They liked to tease me about my southern drawl. After a while this was not funny any more. I could take the sacrifice of leaving the family better than the razzing I often received because I walked slower, talked differently, and did things in different ways."

Leaving Family. This is the second obstacle young women face since 27 percent of the 500 nuns listed this as their major hurdle. For many it means leaving home for the first time, travelling a great distance and remaining away for a long time before getting back for a visit. Here is how a young nun, 21, describes her feelings on the matter:

"Separation from a loving home where life was easy and very comfortable is tough. I remember watching my parents suffer in silence both before

SISTER'S VOCATION OBSTACLES

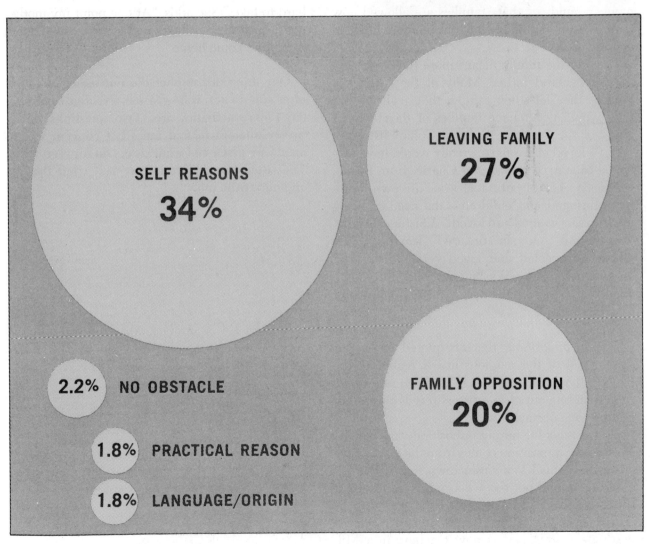

SELF REASONS
34%

LEAVING FAMILY
27%

2.2% NO OBSTACLE

1.8% PRACTICAL REASON

1.8% LANGUAGE/ORIGIN

FAMILY OPPOSITION
20%

About 13 percent of the sisters do not offer obstacles
they faced upon entering the convent.

I left and during the first year. I had come to realize that, at seventeen, I still had a lot of maturing to do."

This young lady seems to have grown up quite a bit since she is now a full time college student living at a convent in Manhattan. She will take her final vows at the age of 25.

Leaving home meant home-sickness for many of the sisters and they readily admit this in the survey. Also, many of them admit they were actually afraid to tell their parents about their desire to enter the convent.

For other sisters it was just plain "leaving a family whom I loved dearly," as it is expressed by a 23-year-old teaching Sister from San Antonio, Texas. However, a Sister of Mercy from Barr, Vermont, reminds us that "families are allowed now to enter more intimately into our religious life than ever before."

Leaving the family means more than just leaving mother and father. Many of the sisters say that, as they left their family, they realized that they would never have families of their own. A Sister of the Precious Blood in Columbus, Ohio, says, "I loved children so I really would have preferred to marry." A Sister of Charity from Boone, Iowa, says her big obstacle was "my own desire for a husband and children — the need of being made to feel wanted and loved." A Sister in Seattle, Washington, said she dreaded "leaving a boy whom I respected and loved very much." And another in Spokane, Washington, said "the knowledge that I could not be a mother, was my most difficult obstacle."

Family opposition, that oft-quoted reason for staying out of the religious life, is really not the bane to the sisterhood that it has been said to be. Less than one out of five sisters recalls this as her number one obstacle.

The reasons for family opposition vary widely. Most of the opposition comes from the father. One father in a small Wisconsin town feared that his daughter would not receive a proper education if she entered the convent. This later proved to be untrue since his daughter went on to receive a graduate degree and is now teaching in a Mil-

waukee high school. Another father opposed his daughter's entry into the convent because of the "lack of prestige" of the particular order she was selecting. He would not have opposed his daughter so much if she had chosen a bigger, "more established" community.

On the other hand, mothers have also provided some sisters with formidable opposition. One mother called up a Franciscan Sister regularly during her novitiate years. Not only would she call her daughter and beg her to come home, she also disturbed her daughter's superiors with repeated phone calls and mailed a beautiful set of fashionable clothes to the convent at least every six months to tempt her daughter to leave. The sister comments, "don't think that wasn't a bit hard to take." She adds, "At one point my mother got desperate and threatened to leave the Church if I didn't come home."

One thing this mother did not realize, as most of us still do not, is how sisters live and what their day-to-day activities are. Two questions in the survey attempt to find out what convent assignments are given and what sisters do for recreation. The sisters themselves tell us next what they do on and off the job.

On The Job
And Off

There is work to be done and almost all the sisters who participated in the survey have at least two responsibilities to keep up with. The first job in 90 percent of the cases is teaching; housework for 13 percent; administration for 12.5 percent; studying in college for 9.4 percent; studying or teaching music for 8 percent; sacristy work including altar boy training, sewing vestments and baking altar breads for 6 percent; nursing, library work, writing, publicity, and art for another 6 percent of the sisters.

Many people see the teaching sister as a standard character with little individuality, personality, secret hopes and desires, problems, failures or accomplishments. As one Bernardine Sister from Dallas, Texas, commented, "I would like to be treated like a human being once in a while."

Since 90 percent of the sisters in the survey have a primary function of teaching in parish ele-mentary schools, let us take a look at who she is and what she does.

The teaching sister is coming into greater de-mand. About 80 percent of the Catholic education facilities in the United States are elementary schools and, of the total sister population of about 180,000, only 120,000 are available to teach in them.

Second, the teaching sister is a very busy woman who needs the energies of a mother who manages a large family. Many subtle changes in duties and activities tax the energies of the modern sister.

Some of these subtle changes include the indi-vidualizing of sisters. More and more sisters are determining what it takes to get a job done. There are activities during the day which are optional in the more up-to-date communities. Some of these optional activities, formerly a must for every sister, are daily Mass, certain community prayers, meals at a specified time for everyone, and other regimented programs requiring the participation of every sister in the convent.

Military-like convent schedules are becoming a thing of the past. The individual sister is determining how she should spend her time within the framework of a more casual and relaxed daily schedule. More time is being made available, too, for the individual sister to pursue those things which interest her most, on the job and off.

In a way the modern sister can be compared with a housewife who must also determine how she should manage her time, when to go shopping, and what needs to get done on a particular day. The more relaxed daily schedule of the modern sister requires a greater maturity and professionalism which brings us to the third point.

The teaching sister is a professional person — an educator. She brings to her work a skill and devotion that would make her a good professional in any field. The parish sisters stress academic achievement since they are primarily in the business of education. Only 3.5 percent first entered the convent with a college degree already in hand. The majority study for a degree after they enter. About 71 percent of the nuns responding say they now have a college diploma and a third of the remaining 29 percent are now working for theirs.

The teaching sister has a good variety of recreation and is far from being a modern recluse. The forms of recreation mentioned in the survey are mainly creative — music, either listening or performing, singing, reading, art and various handicrafts, dancing, sewing and artistic needlework.

The art of conversation is not lost by any means since 37 percent mention this as their favorite form of recreation. Many mention they enjoy conversations most when they are meaningful and serious discussions. The favorite topic is the children with whom they spend so much time. Like mothers they enjoy telling the funny incidents that happen during the day and perhaps comment now and then about the psychological and social implications of the everyday experiences they have with children.

Their recreation is quite active, too. Outdoor sports are a major recreation for one out of four sisters; one out of five likes to swim. Other more active recreation includes hiking, softball, basketball, bowling, volleyball and the whole range of indoor and outdoor sports.

For the busy sister it is not all fun and games because she does not find enough time to do her job and recreate too. A Dominican Sister reminds us that "favorite recreational activities are not a consistent happening." Another says that "recreational activities in this age of hurry and flurry are not what I would deem conducive to freedom from tension and excessive activities. Discussions and conversations within the community have long since lost their relaxation character because of our great workloads." So many, like the Holy Cross Sister from Texas, would "like to look forward to the time when sisters will be free to recreate more and to bowl and play tennis and swim without a picture of this activity being printed in every newspaper."

Like most people today, sisters are extremely busy women—who want to be looked upon as all other busy professionals, not as curiosities. You might wonder whether or not they would encourage others to join them in their unique position in today's society. They do encourage young women to consider convent careers but they offer four practical points of advice. Let's see what they are in the next chapter.

SISTER OCCUPATIONS

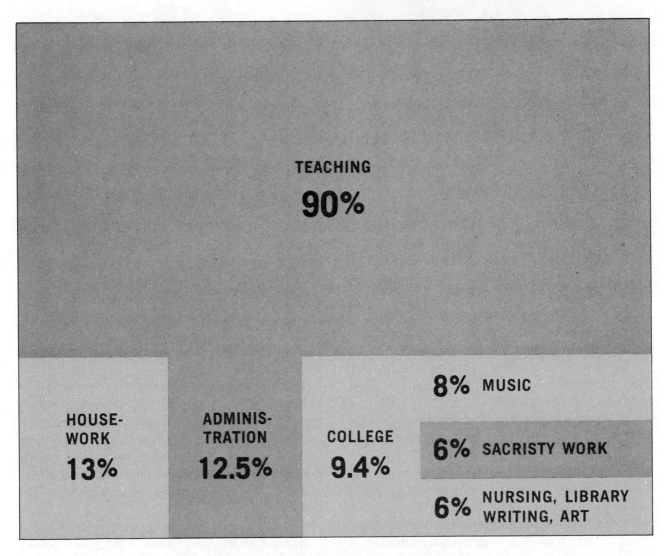

TEACHING

90%

HOUSE-WORK

13%

ADMINIS-TRATION

12.5%

COLLEGE

9.4%

8% MUSIC

6% SACRISTY WORK

6% NURSING, LIBRARY WRITING, ART

Over half of the 500 respondents named two principal occupations which keep them busy during the week thus bringing percentage totals to 144.9%. Since the survey covered parish convents only, it explains the high percentage of teaching occupations compared with the others.

Advice To Young Women

"Be brave! I think courage is the most important virtue in life for any young woman, especially one about to enter the convent."

"Be certain this is what you want before you take the step. Don't let anyone else talk you into it or talk you out of it."

"Don't wait for a bolt of lightning from heaven. Pray and continue your normal social life. Find someone you can talk with."

"Have a regular confessor and spiritual director and be sure to enter a convent that is *up-to-date*."

"Pick the religious order carefully."

"Get some experience in the business world and support yourself for at least one year. Be prepared to live with and love difficult people. Some sisters are often narrow-minded, selfish and petty. They need as much patience and understanding as people will need anywhere. There are, however, many wonderful sisters who will help you to understand the miserable ones. We must all strive together to bring all our sisters to have large minds and hearts so that we can work effectively for Christ."

"Enjoy life, give it all you have, and then give it all to God."

These random bits of advice are as applicable to boys as they are to girls. The advice that sisters give, offers a general yardstick for measuring, by percentage of mentions, those ideas concerning what is important to think about. They could, perhaps, be summed up in the words of a Franciscan Sister in Granville, Iowa, who says "Be yourself."

Know Yourself. 45 percent of the sisters would first advise young women or any young person considering a career to enjoy life, get to know yourself, live a little, but don't go off the deep end. Convent life is one for adults. "It's not kid stuff." Every other sister would recommend growing up first before even considering a convent career. For some that might mean going to college or working until they are 21, 25, or even 30 years old. Most of the problems of convent life are concerned with other people and dealing with them demands a maturity and a human understanding as solid and deep as any profession or career, including marriage.

A Sister in Burlington, Iowa, warns that the convent "has no room for the small-souled person." A Franciscan Sister who took her final vows ten years ago writes:

"Do not enter as an escape or form the idea of a peaceful bed of roses — one in which everything comes your way. Work to build a well-rounded personality before entering."

A principal of an elementary school in Rochester, New York, urges girls not to enter immediately after high school. "Girls don't know themselves well enough to take this step for life," she states. "We say girls are not old enough to marry at seventeen and I say they are not old enough to take this big step in their lives."

A principal of a high school in Waterloo, Iowa, offers some ideas on how young women might get to know themselves better. She writes: "Complete high school before entering religious life. Have dates with a good number of boys. Travel to other states. Learn how to manage your income. If you can, get a part-time job in high school. Learn to demonstrate interest in others by going out of your way to meet and speak with others of all faiths and races."

"It's love all the way," says an eighth grade sister and teacher from Petersham, Massachusetts. "One must like people and be able to smile at them on rainy days, to communicate with them and to laugh at yourself — others will anyway."

Prayer Program. Over a third of the sisters feel that young women considering a convent career should have a regular program of prayer. Set up a schedule that is convenient and helpful. Don't just

WHAT A GIRL
SHOULD KNOW

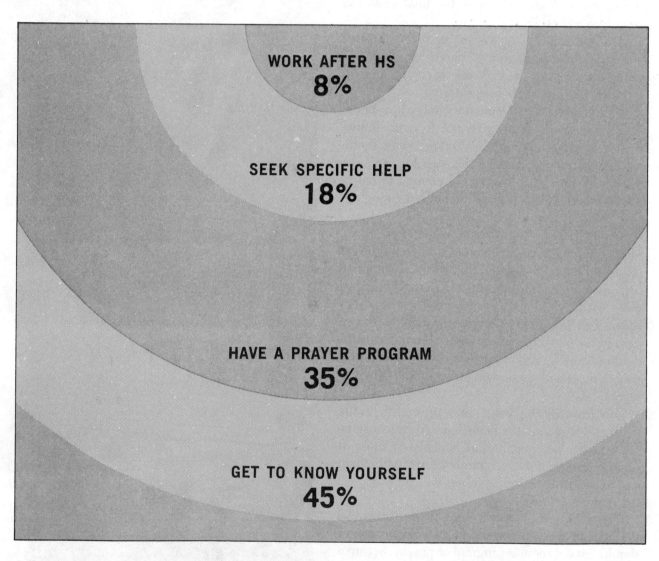

WORK AFTER HS
8%

SEEK SPECIFIC HELP
18%

HAVE A PRAYER PROGRAM
35%

GET TO KNOW YOURSELF
45%

A few sisters offer more than one kind of advice,
bringing the total to 106 percent.

pray for yourself, but as one Franciscan Sister suggests, "Pray for an increase of human faith and loving generosity on the part of everyone."

Having the benefit of someone else's considered advice is also important. If possible, regular visits to a priest or sister confidant would be a great help. A Sister of Providence who took her final vows last year at age 30 advises, "Pray seriously, think deeply, complete perhaps all of college, seek advice from priests, sisters or others considered to be men and women of integrity and high Christian ideals."

When you do seek the advice of others, cautions a Benedictine music teacher from St. Mary's, Pennsylvania, "Be open with your confessor or spiritual director; speak frankly and don't play word games."

Another Pennsylvania sister who teaches and acts as principal in a suburban parish lists prayer at the top of her list of advice. Here is her list of four points:

1. Pray over the thought before jumping.
2. Be informed about all major items.
3. Know life is hard if you make it that way.
4. Love is very important. You must have experience with it — love of father and mother and good relationships with others. This is love.

Seek Help. Some 18 percent of the sisters think along fairly practical lines. Their comments can be summarized as "Don't take everything on faith, hope and charity; do something about it yourself."

A 25-year-old sister who teaches in Jennings, Louisiana, believes a young lady must be selective. "Be sure," she writes, "that you realize what type of apostolic work you will be engaged in beforehand and then find a community that offers what you would like."

Another 25-year-old sister teaching in Billings, Montana, says the same thing, but adds reassuringly that she is not the least bit disappointed with her choice. She advises, "First, choose your community with care — some are very backward." Then she says, "Be prepared to accept many frustrations in people and activities, but, more positively, develop a real love for and patience with and tact toward all kinds of people."

"Nuns are not angels; they're people," one sister reminds us.

To underline the need to be practical about selecting the right religious community, a St. Agnes Sister from the Bronx, New York, reflects: "The Church is moving ahead — find a community which is alive with the spirit of the Church and which has adapted to bringing the Gospel to the 20th century man."

Get a Job. Another practical bit of advice from one out of twelve sisters in the survey is to get a job after high school. A Maryknoll Sister, still under 30 years of age, thinks every girl should be "at least partially working for her own financial needs."

If a girl does not go to college, there is more reason for her to work after high school. Many of the sisters who suggest working a while, feel that a year or two in the business world will make one a better sister. While working at a job, many mention that it would be a good idea to become involved in "some type of social apostolate."

To sum up the advice to girls, the sisters are saying: get to know yourself and get as much experience as you can before entering the convent. They are also saying, "Choose carefully; it is a solid life of mature decision."

Another young sister asks these questions:

1. Have you ever been in a convent kitchen or living quarters?
2. Do you know how they put on their habit?
3. Have you ever chatted with a nun over a coke or a cup of coffee?
4. Have you ever had a meal with a nun in or outside the convent?

"If your answer is NO to any of these questions, you haven't learned enough of what convent life is all about."

It might be a good idea for parents to visit a convent, chat over coffee or dine with a religious. Not only would these encounters create better understanding, but they might eliminate the need for many of the comments priests and sisters have for parents. This advice for fathers and mothers is contained in the next chapter.

Advice To Parents

"Think more of your daughter than you do of yourself."

"Religious life is a tremendous love."

"Don't panic; a religious can be 'fulfilled' too."

"Say: 'Goodbye, God bless you! We are proud and will pray for you.'"

"Keep lines of communication open."

"Very often parents see religious life as a turning away from the world, when in reality it is a turning to God through a total commitment to his world."

Our survey question for parents reads: I would offer the following advice to parents of those girls (or young men) who are contemplating entering the religious life:

At one time or another every Catholic parent might be faced with an expression of interest on the part of one or more daughters in the religious life, a feeling that it is attractive to them. The survey reveals that 20 percent of the parents actively discourage or oppose a son's or daughter's consideration of a religious career. They do so for a variety of reasons — protectiveness, selfishness, lack of conviction about their own faith and many other reasons. Some parents feel religious life is a stilted, narrow kind of existence.

One grade-school sister in Wisconsin relates, "My father was reluctant because of his fear that I would not be educated."

What should parents do if and when a son or daughter expresses some interest in the religious life? The priests and sisters who responded to the survey offer a number of suggestions which fall into twelve major categories. The responses contain a number of "key words" which are tabulated and grouped. The percentages indicate how often the same kind of advice to parents appears in the responses.

Encouragement. The most important thing parents can do is to show interest, encouragement and support, according to 46 percent of the sisters. This type of advice ranges from a passive or detached approach to active, enthusiastic encourage-

14

ment which might border on pushing. Most of the priests and religious who offer this advice, however, believe parents should remain impartial.

"Encourage but don't be either pushy or bitter," writes a Sister of Charity from Iowa.

"Give them the generous support required in any life undertaking," says a St. Joseph Sister from West Virginia.

Her associate from the same convent in West Virginia adds, "Encourage by being available when she wants to talk things over."

"R-E-L-A-X! Be a good listener," a Benedictine from Kansas cautions, "and assure her of your interest and desire to help when you can."

"Treat your daughter as you would if she were interested in nursing, teaching or any other professional career," one of the Presentation of Mary Nuns advises.

Her Own Decision. About 23 percent of the priests and nuns recommend that parents let their son or daughter make his or her own decision. All of the advisers who make this point specifically mention or stress the words, "own decision." Here are some examples:

"Let the decision be the daughter's as much as possible," a young nun in Milwaukee admonishes.

And another from St. Paul puts it, "Be generous and let your daughter try this life."

"Leave the final decision to the boy himself, giving him prudent encouragement, assuring him that they are interested in his entering a vocation, any vocation, in which he will be able to help others and perfect himself — no pressure," writes a priest journalist from the St. Cloud diocese.

"The decision is hers to make before God," a 26-year-old Ursuline from Texas urges, "but let her know that you are behind her whatever her decision."

Pray. The same number of priests and sisters, 23 percent, offer spiritual advice for parents. They say pray. Pray for yourself and for your son or daughter. Pray for the right decision, the right attitude and the right religious order.

"Stop pushing and start praying," writes a sister from Dubuque who apologized because she lost her questionnaire "in the pile of unpaid bills which kept growing."

"Pray and give your son a happy home life," advises a rural pastor from the Fargo diocese.

A Marian Nun from Nebraska reminds parents they should support their daughter's decision, whatever it is, through prayer.

Priority. Another spiritual approach the sisters take in their advice is a not-so-subtle reminder that God owns their daughter, not the parents. About one out of six sisters counsel that God has the priority and that it's God's call to the convent.

A Dominican teaching Sister from Oshkosh cautions, "Christ is calling! If you put an obstacle in your daughter's way, be careful of whose way you are getting into."

"Parents, your children were given to you by God," reminds a 23-year-old professed of the Incarnate Word and Blessed Sacrament order, "and you never have to worry about the spiritual or temporal walfare of your daughter if God calls her."

"You will never be sorry if it is what God wants," says a sister from Atchison.

Understand. Discuss and try to understand in every possible way is the advice of ten percent of the priests and sisters who suggest that parents be available to discuss and examine motives as realistically as possible. "The joys and hardships of the choice must be examined."

A Sister of Mercy from Vermont declares, "Try to understand the desire of your child and see the life of consecrated service as worthwhile."

A Benedictine high school counsellor in Arkansas urges, "Be generous — a vocation is a mystery and also a very personal thing."

While understanding, discussion and reasoning may be advisable according to ten percent, some of these sisters, like the one from Loretto, Colorado, say "slow down." "Don't try to probe too deeply into all the reasons why your daughter would want to be a religious; she may not know herself."

Understanding involves attitude. A Divine Providence Sister writes, "You cannot change cir-

cumstances surrounding your daughter's desire, but you can change attitudes."

"Approach the issue with a positive viewpoint," a nun from Pittsburgh suggests. She became a nun in 1963 in spite of what was a great obstacle — "strong family bonds."

Understanding has to be shown, according to an Indiana nun who writes, "Show a *genuine* love and appreciation for the religious life." Misunderstanding must not be shown in ways as another Indiana Franciscan indicates, "Don't expect your daughter to act like a pious girl from the moment she mentions she would like to become a nun, but encourage her to enjoy life."

Along the same line, parents should keep in mind that their daughter is human, just like they are. A School Sister of Notre Dame from Minnesota expresses this point with a warning:

"Make it clear to your daughter what the laity expect and want to find in a religious — a human being, not a plaster saint! Alert her to the possibility of having her human warmth and sparkle drummed out of her by Jansenistic or puritanical training, and if such is the 'spirit of the order,' she should have the courage to leave."

A final note on understanding comes from a

63-year-old pastor in the Diocese of Superior. He admonishes, "Make sure your own ideals of the priesthood are sound; then help to reach for them."

About ten percent of the priests and sisters responding to the survey offer no advice for parents. One nun commented that advice should depend on particular circumstances and that in her opinion generalized advice was of little value.

Investigate. About one out of ten advise some practical steps for parents to take. This group says investigate, look into it and satisfy yourself that religious careers are okay. An Ursuline from Galveston suggests that parents should meet the mothers and fathers of religious to discuss their experiences when daughter decides to enter the convent. Others bring up ideas such as visiting convents, seminaries or provincial houses in the community. This can be done by appointment or on days when they have open house which can be learned by a quick phone call. Another idea is to write mother-houses of different orders to find out about their particular programs. Addresses are given in any standard Catholic directory available in most parish libraries.

The priests and nuns indicate that selection of

the right religious order for your daughter can be an important factor and choice should not be based on convenience or happenstance. Better yet, according to some of them, have your son or daughter investigate by writing various religious orders that interest them. They say it doesn't make sense, for example, for your daughter to enter a teaching order if she is interested in nursing or an austere cloistered society if she has up-to-date motives for dedicating her life. A few mention that you should send your son or daughter "for advice to some uninvolved party" and make sure he or she has frequent contact and association with priests or nuns before making the move to enter.

Be proud. In their advice to parents some nine percent are of the happy and proud persuasion. They say be proud. Be happy. Share in your son's or daughter's joy and anticipation.

Grow Up. About nine percent are in the "grow up" group. They ask parents to help their son or daughter mature a little before entering religious life. One from Hershey, Pennsylvania, advises completion of high school and at least a year in the business world to get a little maturity before entering. Another from Bartlesville, Oklahoma, writes, "DON'T shelter them, let them get around to see what life is all about."

Another idea in the maturity area comes from a teaching Sister of Christian Charity in Wisconsin. She says, "Encourage your daughter to get interested and active in Y.C.S. (Young Christian Students) or any such social action group — local, national or international."

Family Life. Continue your exemplary family life is the advice mentioned by five percent. They feel your son or daughter would not be interested in religious life if your family were not already pretty great. A sister from Dubuque seconds the idea with, "keep showing the beauty of love in your home."

To a priest from Montana, good family life includes "lots of family give and take with lots of self reliance, too." A Perpetual Adoration Sister from Idaho Falls, Idaho, adds that good family atmosphere means "the same freedom of expres-

sion of desire and opportunity to carry it out." One sister believes family life is very important for any vocation. She writes:

"The religious vocation begins, before the child enters school, with the family life itself. The home should be a place of reverence and love for the individual, sensitivity for others and complete responsible freedom."

Reward. Only two percent of the priests and sisters responding in the survey hold out any kind of carrot as a reward. Parents will be rewarded in many ways, they say. Parents will be happy for one thing; they won't lose a daughter. "As the years pass, she will be closer than ever to you," states a Sister of St. Agnes from Victoria, Kansas.

Parents will not get grandchildren from the vocation-child, a nun reminds us, but they will "remain primary in the affections and prayers of the daughter because she won't have husband and children of her own to think about." A priest thinks the long term rewards for parents are huge but "the resulting joys are not in immediate view."

Then there are about two percent who hold up the "keep out" sign to parents. "Don't interfere in any way. Stay out of it entirely." "Keep your fears to yourselves."

A young parish priest from the Sioux Falls diocese observes, "The qualifications for the priesthood are basically no different from those required of a good husband and father. You need educate him no differently in virtue."

A Marian sister from Nebraska reminds parents, "Remember, you were in love once and so is your daughter." Hopefully all parents of nuns and young candidates for the seminary are still in love. Many priests and sisters mention love in their survey responses. One, a 25-year-old Irish immigrant of the Poor Sisters of Nazareth, summarizes all her reasons for becoming a sister simply, "I'm in love, tremendously in love with Christ."

This tremendous love can be helped or hindered depending upon your son's or daughter's relationship to a particular group. Let's see what a sister-psychiatrist has to say about that in the next chapter.

A Practical Approach

Throughout the comments from priests, brothers and sisters, a single bit of advice for those contemplating the religious life and for their parents repeats itself frequently — look into things, investigate, be selective, find out. This theme, itself, warrants further consideration so a prominent psychiatrist, a Sister of Mercy, was asked about the age-old problem of individual vs. group as it pertains to religious communities. The following reports a professional point of view which might clarify the need for being as careful in selecting a religious career as others are in choosing a profession in business or science.

Doctor, what is unique about religious "organizations" vs. others?
Religious vocation directors and others involved in the direction of religious organizations are all concerned with a reappraisal and a restatement of their objectives. The religious communities of men and women and the diocesan authorities across the country all have one big advantage in common, that is, their potential staff members — priests, brothers, and sisters — are people "who have decided to answer an invitation to dedicate their lives in a special way."

The difference among all these organizations lies in their specific, basic objectives. In business, for example, not all organizations are manufacturing companies. Some are distributing organizations. Others are support and service agencies, and many other types make up what is known as the "business community." In the same way, a particular religious community or organization offers an individual, who has decided to accept an

invitation to dedicate his life, a particular external structure which will help carry out this dedication.

Isn't the word, "organization," rather cold and impersonal?

The word "organization" seems to be a cold term to describe religious groups. They would rather refer to themselves as "communities" or "orders" to reflect the totality of their purpose. Yet, many of the comments of priests, brothers and sisters in

the survey reflect their particular feelings about not what should be done, but the way in which goals or objectives should be achieved.

The words, "community" and "order," really mean "organization." Human beings are need-fulfilling, goal-achieving entities and one of the best ways for them to fulfill their needs and achieve their goals is to organize themselves. Mature human beings realize that it is by being a part of a human organization that they can achieve any sort of personal satisfaction and accomplish a meaningful goal at the same time.

Many sisters in the survey expressed the same thought in much the same way. Some were positive like "I decided to become a sister because I felt I could accomplish more through a structured program." And negatively another has confessed, "My biggest obstacle was obtaining recognition as an individual."

Yet, religious communities, orders and congregations are organizations because by definition they are organized to achieve a common goal. An organization is "a unified group of individuals who work together inter-dependently to achieve a common goal while at the same time satisfying individual needs and goals."

How would you describe religious organizations?

Religious organizations are social organizations, because they consist of people. No religious organization expects its members to be identical. It is against human nature. Any person who enters the seminary or the convent must have some idea as to the values and beliefs held by the particular organization, some thoughts as to its nature, works and goals and, last but not least, a clear idea regarding his or her position and standing within the group.

What freedom of choice does a prospective religious have?

Joining a religious organization has been not unlike enlisting in the Army for a lifetime career. At the time of enlistment a young recruit can indicate several areas of interest in which he feels he could be happy as a soldier. Yet there are countless stories about mechanics ending up as cooks and executives being transformed into infantrymen. Convents and religious houses are also filled with similar instances where individual desires were not met because of one reason or another.

People with prior professional training have no guarantee they will be able to operate in the same field once they enter a religious organization. One Maryknoll Sister who has had five years of experience as a physical therapist before she entered, relates that she is only recently being encouraged to take up this profession again. She has been in the Maryknoll organization for ten years. Another sister who gave up a career as a medical technician is now teaching second grade in a small town parish school. She is not complaining, but merely pointing out a common phenomenon of those in religious life.

Is this phenomenon unique with religious organizations?

This phenomenon is common in any life. Very few college graduates, except engineers, doctors and lawyers and perhaps a few others, are working in a field for which they were specifically trained. The lay man or woman can change his job if he later finds out that a particular organization does not suit his or her needs or is not conducive to achieving individual goals. In religious life this is not so. A priest can be "incardinated" into a diocese from a religious order. The Catholic press contains many stories of diocesan priests who for any number of reasons change dioceses but rarely is it possible for a priest, brother or sister to leave one religious order and join another.

What can a prospective religious do about this?

He or she can be as careful and selective as possible by inquiring, visiting and investigating beforehand. It is extremely important for any person who has accepted an invitation to dedicate his life for a religious purpose to choose the right organization at the outset.

What are some of the qualities a prospective religious should have?

Those who enter any religious organization must possess the potential for developing a vision for the organization as well as for themselves. They must know their limitations and see how they fit within the group. They must have the ability for encouraging and cooperating with other members of the group in an imaginative and creative way. The necessity for these qualities cannot be overstressed. Religious organizations need men and women of character, of heroic virtue and tremendous love. The potential religious person must be able to operate in an atmosphere that will satisfy individual needs as well as the objectives of the organization itself. This cannot be done unless the individual has the basic human abilities and some assurances that these abilities will be allowed to develop to their fullness.

How mature should a potential religious be before entering?

The candidate for religious life should be one who has already satisfied basic human needs. It should be one who has already lived with sufficient food, shelter, love, security and who is able to respond to the higher needs of his human nature, that is to become a whole and well-rounded person. In other words, a candidate should be as grown up as possible according to the many, many comments of sisters and brothers who offer advice in the survey. An adult is one who sees his or her abilities and his or her limitations realistically. An adult is one who looks at religious life clearly and honestly, understanding its meaning and understanding its difficulties and tolerating individual limitations in those around him.

Can one who has never had love and security be free enough to give love and security in religious life? Can one whose basic needs have never been fulfilled, fulfill them for others? Can we ask a person not intellectually adequate to lead others to the highest, most sublime truth? How can religious organizations ask this of individuals if they have not experienced and fulfilled these basic needs at home? Without this home background will they have the potential for developing themselves further in any circumstances, much less in religious life?

What does the religious organization owe the new member?

The young person who enters religious life enters an organization which promises to give that person an opportunity to achieve a goal of perfection by working within a particular group. The organization promises it will enable such an individual to achieve the major goals provided some secondary needs are given up for the common good. There are four practical ways of looking ahead in order to select the "right" religious or-

ganization. (There are over 300 separate religious organizations for women in the United States, over 150 religious organizations for men and about that many dioceses to choose from!)

What should one do first to select a religious organization?

1. Learn as much as you can about the organization ahead of time. Every religious organization has a constitution which reflects the image of its particular group as a whole. Its constitution is the distinguishing document that makes one organization different from the other.

2. Each organization has basic resources (human, material, philosophical, spiritual) which have a bearing on the activities of the entire organization. These resources are collected together in a certain climate which is helpful toward achieving its goals. Find out what these are. Is the organization on a sound financial basis? Is it successful thus far in accomplishing its stated objectives? Be careful not to evaluate any organization in terms of numbers and material success alone.

3. Learn about the activities of the organization, activities surrounding the acquiring, maintaining and using of all the resources it has, especially philosophical and spiritual. Compare how it recruits and trains its candidates. Do you feel comfortable with the approach? Is the approach guarded and defensive or is it open and free? Examine these things as you pursue your investigations.

4. Examine how all of the above are brought together to fulfill the needs of those already in the organization and how this is contributing to the achievement of organization goals. This can best be done by spending some time visiting various religious houses, talking with various members, not once but several times before you decide. Once you have made a decision to dedicate your life to special service as a religious, the question is — in which religious program will you find the greatest fulfillment? For those who have not made the basic commitment, this investigative process should be helpful in reaching a final decision. Either way, it is a beneficial investment of time and effort.

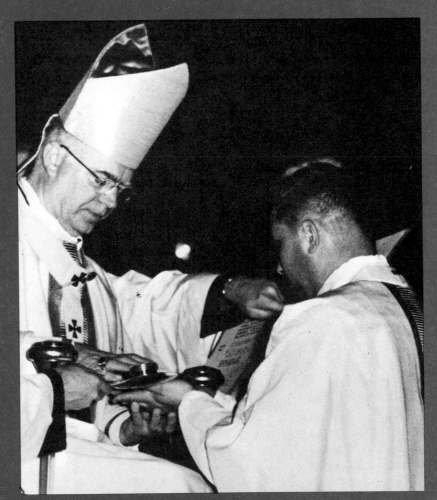

MOST REVEREND JOHN F. DEARDEN, D.D.
Archbishop of Detroit

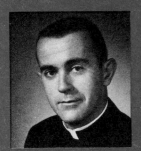

Father Edward Baldwin
Vocation Director

Sister Jane Edward
Associate Director

INVITATION TO ACTION
in the
ARCHDIOCESE OF DETROIT

"Only those who labor to ransom the present are worthy to inherit the promises of the future. The Church we seek to become depends upon the Church we are today. The Christian responsibility is three-fold: it looks to the past with REVERENCE, to the present with RESPONSI-BILITY, and to the future with FAITH, which is the substance of HOPE."

THE CHURCH IN OUR DAY
By the Catholic Bishops of the U.S. (Jan. 1968)

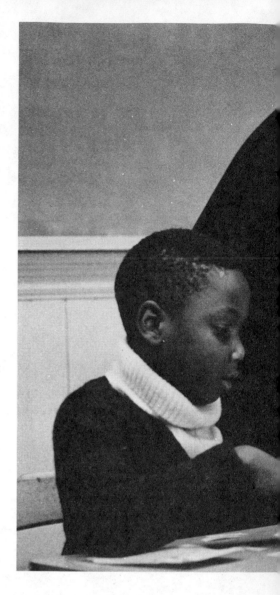

*I became all things
to all men
that I might save all.*

*And I do all things
for the Gospel's sake,
that I may be made
partaker thereof.*

The first Epistle of
St. Paul to the Corinthians, 10:22

A Special Word...

FOR THOSE ACTUALLY READY TO APPLY
AS CANDIDATES FOR THE
PRIESTHOOD — BROTHERHOOD — SISTERHOOD

This book was produced to clearly show the challenges, rewards, obstacles and influences of a religious vocation. It was designed to create a better understanding among all as to the life and dedication of the priest or religious.

It is particularly addressed to those who believe they have a call to the priesthood, sisterhood or brotherhood. For these we extend an invitation to carefully read the following pages for self-appraisal and consider them all carefully.

Answer them all honestly. Review them all carefully. Should you believe the life of a priest, sister or brother is for you, contact the Vocation Office to arrange for a discussion of you and your future. We are here to help and to guide you — to supply information and counsel.

Most Reverend
Walter J. Schoenherr, D.D.
Delegate for Clergy

CONTACT:

Archdiocese of Detroit Vocation Office
305 Michigan Avenue
Detroit, Michigan 48226

Telephone: 963-3680
Extension 367

Father Edward Baldwin
Director of Vocations

Sister Jane Edward
Associate Director

Why not take the time to write down each question and then an answer; even listing in detail the High School and/or College attended, the name of your parish and the groups you have been active in. You might wish to send this report in before a meeting, and if so, please be sure to include your name and address, telephone, birth date and year.

The Vocation...

1. Which vocation are you interested in?

2. When was the first time you began thinking about this vocation? Has the thought of your vocation been of long duration, or only on occasion?

3. Has anyone suggested that you have a vocation? If so, whom and how often? (example: Mother, Father, teacher, priest, sister). Why?

4. What attracts you most to this vocation?

5. What do you fear most about this vocation?

6. In this vocation what do you think you can contribute? (In view of your talents, possible experience, other factors)

7. If given the opportunity, what special work would you like to do in this vocation?

8. The following are obstacles which can prevent one from coming to a definite decision as regards a vocation. Comment on each one as it affects you:

    a. parental opposition
    b. selfishness
    c. inability to make decisions
    d. intellectual incapacity
    e. celibacy
    f. lack of courage
    g. personal spiritual life
    h. other special obstacles in your way

9. Do you think of this vocation as a happy life?

10. Do you think this vocation could make your life more meaningful than some other field of endeavor? Why?

11. In this vocation, what do you think would be the area of your greatest difficulty in being effective?

12. Which particular aspects of this vocation interest you most?

Personal History...

1. How frequently do you go to confession?

2. How frequently do you receive Holy Communion?

3. To whom do you go for help with your personal problems?

4. List any Church activities you have been engaged in.

5. Do you have close personal friends? How many?

6. Have you ever dated?

7. Have you ever been engaged or kept steady company?

8. Do you belong to any clubs or social organizations? Which?

9. What are your hobbies or interests? (Past and Present)

10. Are you at ease in the presence of others?

11. Would you characterize yourself as a person who enjoys helping others?

12. State some instances where you feel you have helped others.

13. If you are a student, what field of endeavor is your present course of study preparing you for?

14. Are you satisfied and content with your present course of study? Why?

15. Have you ever considered other fields of endeavor? State which ones.

16. If you are not a student, what is your present field of endeavor?

17. Are you satisfied and content in your present field of endeavor? Why?

18. List the jobs you have had and indicate how long you spent in each job since you left school.

19. Have you been interested in other fields of endeavor? State which ones.

Education...

Would you describe yourself as a (poor, average, above average) student?

Which subjects did you prefer?

Which subjects did you least prefer?

Did you have any problems in school? (for those interested in the priesthood, did you study Latin? How many years?)

Have you participated in any forms of public speaking, debate, oratory, acting? State which.

Do you like to read? In what particular fields?

List class offices held. List extracurricular activities.

Rate Yourself...

Write down the quality and then follow it with the number that indicates your own appraisal.

(1) **High**   (2) **Above average**   (3) **Average**   (4) **Below average**   (5) **Low**

In self confidence

In making hard decisions

In courtesy

In listening to people

In willingness to accept criticism

In being tactful with people

In personal drive and ambition

In religious practice

In willingness to be taught

In being tolerant of others' shortcomings

In living up to your moral standards

In admitting your own mistakes

In ability to work under pressure

In accuracy of work

In ability to get along with others

In assuming responsibility

In neatness of dress and personal grooming

In controlling your temper

In desire for Vocation

In expressing yourself

In memory for details

In habits of study

In physical health

In outdoor sports

Conscience

In persuading others

In clerical work

APOSTLES OF THE SACRED HEART
Sister Dolorita
121 E. Boston Boulevard
Detroit, Michigan 48202 (873-6681)

SISTERS OF ST. BASIL (Ukranian)
Sister Brigid
3055 Hanley Avenue
Hamtramck, Michigan 48212 (873-5191 872-1962)

* BERNARDINE SISTERS
Sister Margaret Mary
1045 N. Silvery Lane
Dearborn, Michigan 48128 (561-8338 562-9058)

BON SECOURS SISTERS
Sister John Philip
468 Cadieux Road
Grosse Pointe, Michigan 48230 (884-0400)

CARMELITE SISTERS OF THE AGED
Mother Armand Marian
2560 Woodward Avenue
Detroit, Michigan 48201 (963-3545)

CARMELITE SISTERS OF THE
DIVINE HEART OF JESUS
Sister M. Adelberta
4800 Cadieux Road
Detroit, Michigan 48224 (882-3800)

* DISCALCED CARMELITE NUNS
Mother M. Carmel
16630 Wyoming Avenue
Detroit, Michigan 48221 (862-7995)

SISTERS OF CHARITY OF CINCINNATI
Sister Judith
15255 Mayfield
Detroit, Michigan 48205 (371-0741)

SISTERS OF CHRISTIAN CHARITY
Sister Mariata
3157 Sargent Street
Detroit, Michigan 48211 (921-4641 921-0794)

DAUGHTERS OF THE HEART OF MARY
Box 301
Centerline, Michigan

DAUGHTERS OF DIVINE CHARITY
Sister Mary Loretta
1315 North Woodward
Bloomfield Hills, Michigan 48013 (654-1011)

DAUGHTERS OF ST. MARY OF PROVIDENCE
Sister Clare
16115 Beck Road
Northville, Michigan 48167 (GL 3-1300)

DAUGHTERS OF CHARITY OF SVDP
Sister Oliva
29625 Inkster Road
Farmington, Michigan 48024 (566-1558)

DISCIPLES OF THE DIVINE MASTER
Mother M. Patricia
12830 Warren Avenue
Dearborn, Michigan 48126 (582-1181)

SISTERS OF DIVINE PROVIDENCE
Sister Marise
21101 Bournemouth Avenue
Harper Woods, Michigan 48236 (881-3311 881-6620)

* DOMINICAN NUNS OF PERPETUAL ADORATION
Mother Mary of Mercy
29575 Middlebelt Road
Farmington, Michigan 48024 (626-8253)

* DOMINICAN SISTERS OF ADRIAN, MICH.
Sister Christa
1945 Webb Avenue
Detroit, Michigan 48206 (868-6549 868-6855)

DOMINICAN SISTERS OF COLUMBUS, OHIO
Sister Renata
16231 Charlevoix
Grosse Pointe Park, Michigan 48230 (886-1440)

DOMINICAN SISTERS OF GRAND RAPIDS
Sister John Evangelist
9540 Telegraph Road
Taylor, Michigan 48180 (291-1188 291-0247)

DOMINICAN SISTERS OF MEDIA, PA.
Sister Judith
27840 Independence Road
Farmington, Michigan 48024 (474-8126)

* DOMINICAN SISTERS OF OXFORD, MICH.
Sister Susan
975 E. Gardenia Avenue
Madison Heights, Michigan 48071 (541-2233 398-9546)

DOMINICAN SISTERS OF RACINE, WIS.
Sister Emeline
5970 McClellan
Detroit, Michigan 48213 (921-1031 921-4340)

*Mother houses located in this Archdiocese

DOMINICAN SISTERS OF THE SICK POOR
Sister Carol
700 W. Boston Boulevard
Detroit, Michigan 48202 (868-4378)

DOMINICAN SISTERS OF SPRINGFIELD
Sister Alverna
67926 Howard Street
Richmond, Michigan 48062 (727-1517 727-9365)

SISTERS OF ST. DOROTHY
Sister M. Patrello
1241 Rosedale Court
Detroit, Michigan 48211 (867-0301 867-8021)

* FELICIAN SISTERS
Sister Carmeline
36800 Schoolcraft
Livonia, Michigan 48150 (425-2513)

FRANCISCAN SISTERS OF THE ATONEMENT
Sister Jerome
215 E. Commerce Street
Milford, Michigan 48042 (684-4495)

FRANCISCAN SISTERS OF HAMBURG, NY
Sister Mary Armelia
5680 Konkel Street
Detroit, Michigan 48210 (825-5525 825-5577)

FRANCISCANS OF MISHAWAKA, IND.
Sister Eugene Marie
25225 Code Road
Southfield, Michigan 48075 (356-8785 356-6113)

FRANCISCANS OF OLDENBURG, IND.
Sister Mary Ronald
18720 Thirteen Mile Road
Roseville, Michigan 48066 (776-2943 771-4790)

FRANCISCANS OF PERPETUAL ADORATION
Sister Margaret Ann
2775 Red Fox Trail
Troy, Michigan 48084 (642-2954)

FRANCISCANS OF PITTSBURGH, PA.
Sister Joan of Arc
3562 Bagley Avenue
Detroit, Michigan 48216 (826-1450 826-1842)

FRANCISCANS OF SYLVANIA, OHIO
Sister M. Jerome
5866 St. Lawrence Avenue
Detroit, Michigan 48210 (877-9726)

GOOD SHEPHERD SISTERS
Sister M. Ursula
20651 W. Warren
Detroit, Michigan 48223 (271-3050)

* HOME VISITORS OF MARY
Sister Mary Finn
356 Arden Park
Detroit, Michigan 48202 (875-1123)

HOLY FAMILY OF NAZARETH
Sister M. Sophia
15311 Wick Road
Allen Park, Michigan 48101 (928-4727 388-0100)

HOLY NAMES OF JESUS AND MARY
Sister Yvonne
23407 Jefferson Avenue
St. Clair Shores, Michigan 48080 (771-3735 779-2036)

* IMMACULATE HEART OF MARY
Sister Nivard
610 W. Elm Street
Monroe, Michigan 48161 (241-3660)

INSTITUTE OF BLESSED VIRGIN MARY
Sister Mercedes
17302 Glenmore
Detroit, Michigan 48240 (531-8863 532-4764)

ST. JOSEPH SISTERS OF GARFIELD HEIGHTS
Sister Laboure
20200 Kelly Road
Harper Woods, Michigan 48236 (526-0220 526-0221

ST. JOSEPH SISTERS OF NAZARETH
Sister Ann Laffin
22101 Moross Road
Detroit, Michigan 48236 (881-8200)

LITTLE SISTERS OF THE POOR
Sister Patrice
17550 Southfield Road
Detroit, Michigan 48235 (535-4461)

MARIST SISTERS
Sister Monessa
16103 Chesterfield
East Detroit, Michigan 48021 (772-2577 771-9580)

* RELIGIOUS SISTERS OF MERCY
Sister Mary Ruthanne
8600 Eleven Mile Road
Farmington, Michigan 48024 (476-8000)

MEXICAN MISSIONARY CATECHISTS
Sister Enriquita
2330 Vermont Avenue
Detroit, Michigan 48216 (961-0698)

MISSION HELPERS OF SACRED HEART
Sister Gerard
4229 Seminole Avenue
Detroit, Michigan 48214 (923-6122)

NOTRE DAME DE NAMUR SISTERS
Sister Catherine John
20001 Norfolk
Detroit, Michigan 48219 (535-0174 537-2347)

OBLATE SISTERS OF PROVIDENCE
Sister M. Josita
20500 Ilene
Detroit, Michigan 48221 (342-2379)

OL VICTORY MISSIONARY SISTERS
Sister Clement
290 Arden Park
Detroit, Michigan 48202 (875-7970)

RELIGIOUS OF THE SACRED HEART
Mother H. Carey
171 Lake Shore Drive
Grosse Pointe Farms, Michigan 48236 (896-1221)

SISTER SERVANTS OF MARY IMMACULATE
Sister Albina
3883 Clippert Avenue
Detroit, Michigan 48210 (826-1038 825-2168)

SERVITE SISTERS
Sister Mary Doris
4875 Coplin Avenue
Detroit, Michigan 48215 (822-3381 822-9665)

SCHOOL SISTERS OF NOTRE DAME
Sister Mary Edwardine
21537 Park Lane
Grosse Ile, Michigan 48138 (676-1379 676-1377)

SOCIETY OF MARY REPARATRIX
Mother Mary Piancone
17330 Quincy
Detroit, Michigan 48221 (862-7018)

* XAVIER MISSION SISTERS
Sister Lorraine
35750 Moravian Drive
Fraser, Michigan 48026 (293-1225)

Contact person for each community

Communities of Brothers Represented in the Archdiocese of Detroit

BROTHER PATRICK MORRIS
Chairman, Brothers Commission
Archdiocese of Detroit

ORDER OF ST. AUGUSTINE (OSA)
Brother Joachim, OSA
Austin Friary
18210 East Warren Avenue
Detroit, Michigan 48224 (TU 4-0092)

ORDER OF ST. BENEDICT (OSA)
St. Benedict of Montefano
2711 East Drahner Road
Oxford, Michigan 48051 (OA 8-2249)

BROTHERS OF CHRISTIAN INSTRUCTION (FIC)
Brother Stephen, FIC
Mount Assumption
Plattsburgh, New York 12901 (518-561-4031)

Detroit Cathedral High 12
70 West Boston Blvd.
Detroit, Michigan 48202 (868-4624)

CHRISTIAN BROTHERS OF IRELAND (CFC)
Brother E. B. Castellanos, CFC
7101 Lahser Road
Birmingham, Michigan 48010 (MI 7-2526)

CHRISTIAN BROTHERS (FSC)
(Brothers of Christian Schools)
Brother Gabriel, FSC
De La Salle Collegiate High School
11055 Glenfield
Detroit, Michigan 48213 (LA 6-1120)

BROTHERS OF HOLY CROSS (CSC)
Brother Eugene Palinski, CSC
24 West Elm Avenue
Monroe, Michigan 48161 (241-8780)

CONGREGATION OF THE PASSION (CP)
(Passionists)
Reverend Matthew Sullivan CP
St. Paul of the Cross Monastery
23300 Davison Avenue West
Detroit, Michigan 48223 (KE 1-0562)

CAPUCHIN-ORDER OF FRIARS MINOR (OFM Cap)
Brother Leo Wollenweber, OFM Cap
1740 Mt. Elliott Avenue
Detroit, Michigan 48207 (567-5100)

ORDER OF FRIARS MINOR (OFM)
Brother Antonio Xuereb, OFM
20000 West Nine Mile Road
Southfield, Michigan 48075 (444-4388)

ORDER OF FRIARS MINOR CONVENTUAL (OFM Conv)
Province of St. Bonaventure
23755 Military Road
Dearborn Heights, Michigan 48127 (562-1900)

HOLY GHOST BROTHERS (CSSp)
Reverend Hilary J. Kline, CSSp
St. Joseph Novitiate
26260 Thirty Mile Road
Richmond, Michigan 48062 (749-5722)

MARIST BROTHERS (SM)
Notre Dame High School
20254 Kelly Road
Detroit, Michigan 48236 (DR 1-8965)

REDEMPTORIST - CONGREGATION OF
THE MOST HOLY REDEEMER (CSsR)
Brother Richard Charboneau, CSsR
1721 Junction Avenue
Detroit, Michigan 48209 (842-3450)

SOCIETY OF ST. PAUL (SSP)
Brother Marian Santoro
7050 Pinehurst
Dearborn, Michigan 48126 (LU 2-2033)

SOCIETY OF JESUS (SJ)
Brother Arthur K. Dugan, SJ
Colombiere College
Big Lake Road
Clarkston, Michigan 48016 (MA 5-5611)

SONS OF THE SACRED HEART (FSCJ)
Verona Fathers Novitiate
3350 Comboni Way
Monroe, Michigan 48161 (1- CH 2-1274)

OBLATES OF ST. FRANCIS deSALES (OSFS)
Reverend Elmer J. Orosz, OSFS
1116 Iroquois Avenue
Detroit, Michigan 48214 (VA 2-4114)

DIOCESAN SEMINARIES

Very Reverend Addison Wright, S.S., Rector
St. John Provincial Seminary
P. O. 298
Plymouth, Michigan 48170

Right Reverend Monsignor Francis X. Canfield, Rector
Sacred Heart Seminary
2701 Chicago Boulevard
Detroit, Michigan 48206

Very Reverend Walter J. Ziemba, Rector
SS. Cyril and Methodius Seminary
Orchard Lake
Michigan 48034

Communities of Religious Order Priests Represented in the Archdiocese of Detroit

AUGUSTINIAN FATHERS (OSA)
Reverend Dudley Day, OSA
6310 South Claremont Avenue
Chicago, Illinois 60636 (925-1311)

CONGREGATION OF ST. BASIL (CSB)
(Basilian Fathers)
Reverend Edmund M. Brennan, CSB
3990 Giddings Road
Pontiac, Michigan 48057 (388-4551)

SYLVESTRIAN BENEDICTINES (OSB)
(Benedictine Fathers)
Reverend Bartholomew Kraemer, OSB
2711 East Drahner Road
Oxford, Michigan 48051 (OA 8-2249)

ORDER OF FRIARS MINOR CAPUCHIN (OFM Cap)
(Franciscan Fathers, Capuchin)
Reverend Mel Hermanns, OFM Cap
1820 Mt. Elliott Avenue
Detroit, Michigan 48207 (567-5100)

ORDER OF PREACHERS (OP)
(Dominican Fathers)
St. Pius Priory
1909 South Ashland Avenue
Chicago, Illinois 60608

FRIARS MINOR CONVENTUAL (OFM Conv)
(Franciscan Fathers, Conventual)
St. Anthony Monastery
8901 West Vernor
Detroit, Michigan 48209 (VI 1-3377)

ORDER OF FRIARS MINOR (OFM)
(Franciscan Fathers-Province of St. John)
Vocation Director
Duns Scotus College
20000 West Nine Mile Road
Southfield, Michigan 48075 (444-4388)

CONGREGATION OF THE HOLY GHOST (CSSp)
(Holy Ghost Fathers)
St. Joseph Navitiate
Vocation Director
P. O. Box 128
Richmond, Michigan (PI 9-5722)

IMMACULATE HEART OF MARY
MISSION SOCIETY (CICM)
4651 North Twenty-Fifth Street
Arlington, Virginia 22207

SOCIETY OF JESUS (SJ)
(Jesuit Fathers)
Reverend Joseph F. Downey, SJ
892 West Boston Boulevard
Detroit, Michigan 48202 (869-3842)

ST. JOSEPH'S SOCIETY OF THE SACRED HEART (SSJ)
(Josephite Fathers)
Reverend J. Grant Higgins, SSJ
1130 North Calvet Street
Baltimore, Maryland 21202 (SA 7-3386)

MISSIONARIES OF OUR LADY OF LA SALETTE (MS)
Reverend Frank Fitzsimmons MS
2600 Harvard
Berkley, Michigan 48072 (LI 1-3762)

CONGREGATION OF MARIAN
CLERICS REGULAR OF THE
IMMACULATE CONCEPTION (Marian Fathers) (MIC)
1109 Iroquois
Detroit, Michigan 48214 (VA 3-0354)

RELIGIOUS MISSIONARIES OF MARIANNHILL (CMM)
(Mariannhill Mission Society)
St. Bernard Minor Seminary
23601 Ann Arbor Trail
Dearborn Heights, Michigan 48127 (LO 1-8888)

SOCIETY OF MARY (SM)
(Marist Fathers)
Reverend Philip Laplante, SM
27 Isabella Street
Boston, Massachusetts 02117 (HA 6-6460)

MARYKNOLL FATHERS (MM)
Reverend Jeremiah J. Brennan, MM
610 Longfellow Avenue
Detroit, Michigan 48202 (865-0990)

OBLATES OF ST. FRANCIS DE SALES (OSFS)
Reverend E. J. Orosz, OSFS
1116 Iroquois
Detroit, Michigan 48214 (VA 2-4114)

SOCIETY OF THE CATHOLIC APOSTOLATE (SAC)
(Pallottine Fathers)
3352 Fourth Street
Wyandotte, Michigan 48192 (AV 5-2966)

CONGREGATION OF THE PASSION (CP)
(Passionist Fathers)
Reverend Matthew Sullivan, CP
23300 West Davison
Detroit, Michigan 48223 (521-0562)

CONGREGATION OF ST. PAUL THE APOSTLE (CSP)
(Paulist Fathers)
611 West Boston Boulevard
Detroit, Michigan 48202 (TO 8-4700)

PONTIFICAL INSTITUTE FOR
FOREIGN MISSIONS (PIME)
(Missionaries of SS. Peter and Paul)
Reverend Angelo Campagnoli, PIME
9800 Oakland Avenue
Detroit, Michigan 48211 (868-7556)

SOCIETY OF THE PRECIOUS BLOOD (CPPS)
Reverend Frederick Falce, CPPS
4001 Brunnerdale Avenue N. W.
Canton, Ohio 44718 (499-5483)

CONGREGATION OF THE PRIESTS OF THE
SACRED HEART OF JESUS (SCJ)
Reverend Raymond Maher, SCJ
Divine Heart Seminary
Donaldson, Indiana 46513 (936-9920)

CONGREGATION OF THE MOST
HOLY REDEEMER (CSSR)
(Redemptorist Fathers)
Reverend Robert Hirsch, CSSR
1721 Junction
Detroit, Michigan 48209 (842-3450)

SERVITE FATHERS (OSM)
Reverend Brendan M. LaFave, OSM
425 Hillside Avenue
Hillside, Illinois 60162 (ES 8-4776)

SULPICIAN FATHERS (SS)
Very Reverend Addison Wright, S. S.
St. John Provincial Seminary
P. O. Box 298
Plymouth, Michigan 48170 (GL 3-6200)

SONS OF THE SACRED HEART (FSCJ)
(Verona Fathers)
Reverend Joseph Valente, FSCJ
3350 Comboni Way
Monroe, Michigan 48161 (242-1274)

"Only those who labor to ransom the present are worthy to inherit the promises of the future. The Church we seek to become depends upon the Church we are today. The Christian responsibility is three-fold: it looks to the past with REVERENCE, to the present with RESPONSIBILITY, and to the future with FAITH, which is the substance of HOPE."

The Church in Our Day
by the Catholic Bishops of the U.S.

Prayer for Vocations...

Father,
   send into the fields
     the workers
   who will achieve the harvest of tomorrow
     and
   prove their love
     in determined hours
   not counting moments, years,
     unless to note the joy of service
   for others not our own
     but yours
   Grant this
     generation of opportunity
      the vision
     of those whose tomorrows
      depend on the response
       this generation
      makes today
Help us to hear your Son.
     He says to our generation too:
Come follow me.
amen.